Mark Ravenhill

Plays for Young People

Citizenship
Scenes from Family Life
Totally Over You

Mark Ravenhill was born in Haywards Heath, West Sussex, in 1966. Literary Manager of Paines Plough between December 1995 and June 1997, he was appointed Artistic Associate at the National Theatre in the summer of 2002. His first full-length play, *Shopping and Fucking*, produced by Out of Joint and the Royal Court Theatre, opened at the Royal Court Theatre Upstairs in September 1996. His other works include *Faust is Dead* (national tour, 1997); *Sleeping Around*, a joint venture with three other writers (Salisbury Playhouse, 1998); *Handbag* (Lyric Hammersmith Studio, 1998); *Some Explicit Polaroids* (Theatre Royal, Bury St Edmunds, 1999); *Mother Clap's Molly House* (National Theatre, 2001); *Totally Over You* (National Theatre, 2003); *Product* (Traverse Theatre, Edinburgh, 2005); *The Cut* (Donmar Warehouse, London, 2006); *Citizenship* (National Theatre, 2006); *pool (no water)* (Lyric Hammersmith, 2006); *Shoot / Get Treasure / Repeat* (Edinburgh Festival, 2007, awarded both the Fringe First and Spirit of the Fringe Awards); *A Life in Three Acts* (with Bette Bourne; Traverse Theatre, Edinburgh, 2009; winner of both a Fringe First and Herald Archangel Award; Soho Theatre, London, 2010); *Over There* (Royal Court Theatre, 2009); and *Nation* (based on the novel by Terry Pratchett; Olivier, National Theatre, 2009).

D0369629

MARK RAVENHILL

Plays for Young People

Citizenship
Scenes from Family Life
Totally Over You

with an introduction by the author

Methuen Drama

METHUEN DRAMA

1 3 5 7 9 10 8 6 4 2

This collection first published in Great Britain in 2010
by Methuen Drama

Methuen Drama
A & C Black Publishers Limited
36 Soho Square
London W1D 3QY
www.methuendrama.com

Citizenship first published by Methuen Drama in 2006
Copyright © Mark Ravenhill 2006

Scenes from Family Life first published by Faber & Faber
in *New Connections* in 2008. Copyright © Mark Ravenhill 2008

Totally Over You first published by Faber & Faber
in *Shell Connections* in 2003. Copyright © Mark Ravenhill 2008

Introduction copyright © Mark Ravenhill 2010

Mark Ravenhill has asserted his rights under
the Copyright, Designs and Patents Act, 1988,
to be identified as the author of these works

ISBN 978 1 408 12861 9

A CIP catalogue record for this book is available from the British Library

Typeset by Country Setting, Kingsdown, Kent
Printed and bound in Great Britain by CPI Cox & Wyman, Reading, Berkshire

Contents

Mark Ravenhill
Chronology

September 1996   *Shopping and Fucking*, Out of Joint and the
Royal Court Theatre (Royal Court
Theatre Upstairs and national tour)

April 1997   *Faust is Dead*, Actors' Touring Company
(Lyric Hammersmith Studio and national
tour)

February 1998   *Sleeping Around*, a joint venture with three
other writers (Salisbury Playhouse, trans-
ferred to the Donmar Warehouse and
national tour)

September 1998   *Handbag*, Actors' Touring Company
(Lyric Hammersmith Studio and national
tour)

September 1999   *Some Explicit Polaroids*, Out of Joint (New
Ambassadors Theatre and national tour)

May 2000   *North Greenwich*, Paines Plough (Wild
Lunch series)

August 2001   *Mother Clap's Molly House* (Lyttelton,
National Theatre, transferred to the
Aldwych Theatre, February 2003)

July 2003   *Totally Over You*, performed as part of
'Shell Connections' Youth Theatre
Festival (National Theatre)

March 2004   *Moscow* (Royal Court International
Playwrights' Season)

October 2004   *Education*, read as part of 'National
Headlines' season of topical verbatim
monologues (National Theatre)

August 2005   *Product*, Paines Plough (Traverse Theatre,
Edinburgh, and international tour)

Introduction

What does a playwright want when they write a play? To offer something to the world that will be of value, that will last, that will create a significant moment for the audience to remember.

This dream is a long way from the manner in which most plays are received. The audience come in to the theatre from a busy day at work, have a drink and sit through the play. They smile a bit or frown a bit and then go home and get on with their lives. The audience might enjoy the play but will it have any impact on their lives? Hardly at all.

And the actors, who've come together and worked so intensely on your play, will move on once the play closes. They will find new work in another play or on film and television. The lines, the moves, the characters from your play will soon be forgotten as the actors give themselves over to somebody else's script.

All that work for the playwright to write a play, but everyone involved – audience and cast – will probably remain totally unchanged by the experience.

How different if you write for teenage actors and a teenage audience. Teenagers are at a point in their lives when they are finding out who they are. They are trying on different identities for size: playing with different clothes or hair, different emotional states and sexualities. Music, books or theatre can really matter to a teenager – they never know which band or which writer is going to give them that elusive sense of who they are and to which tribe they belong. There's a real chance that if you can find the right story, create the right characters and find the right language that a play will have a profound effect upon a teenager.

The memories of songs or poems or plays listened to or learnt during those teenage years are likely to stay with us for the rest of our lives. Ask an actor if they can remember the lines of the play they were in last month and the chances are that they can't. But ask them about the first play that they were in at school or at youth theatre and you'll soon find them reciting huge chunks of the text and acting out the moves.

The playwright who writes for the professional stage will at some stage be confronted by an uncomfortable truth. The audience we have in our head might be diverse: we might picture the community coming together to see our play. But the truth is that most theatres play to an older, metropolitan and professional audience, a tiny fraction of the community. But there's the real possibility that if you can get a play for teenagers published in a book like this one, you will reach a much wider audience. There are youth theatre and school productions all over the country. They have audiences of family and friends, who may never go to a professional theatre, who will see your play. A play for teenagers can speak to all sorts of people in all sorts of communities and that's why I'm proud of these plays.

So you see, I didn't write these plays as a gesture of goodwill or as a charitable social act. The urge to write them sprang directly from my artist's ego and the wish that my plays have the biggest possible impact on the biggest possible group of people.

I wrote the plays over six years. Looking back at them now, they make up a loose trilogy. The first one I wrote was *Totally Over You*. There's an innocence and playfulness about the characters in this play. Kitty and Jake are young teenagers with all the volatile emotions of young people experiencing love for the first time. This is reflected in the form of the play, which takes an old plot from Molière's *Les Precieuses Ridicules* and re-imagines it in a school setting. Tom and Amy in *Citizenship* are a bit older than Jake and Kitty, preparing themselves for a world after they've left school and realising that sex and sexuality are infinitely complex. The play draws more on the traditions of social realism and soap opera, with the occasional slip into the fantastical. Jack and Lisa in *Scenes from Family Life* are, like Tom and Amy, a year or so after leaving school and with a young baby on the way. But the world they inhabit is very different from that of *Citizenship*. The world of this last play draws more on the Absurdist plays of Beckett and Ionesco, plays that I enjoyed as a teenager.

I hope you will put these plays on at your school or youth theatre. I didn't write them so that that they could be read: they are intended entirely for performance. None of them needs very much in the way of special costumes or scenery. You should be able to find any of the props you need without too much difficulty. The cast sizes are intended to be about right for the average drama class or youth group and I've tried to introduce some crowd scenes in which the numbers can be flexible. There's nothing particularly needed in the way of lighting or sound effects. (Lots of different groups have played around with ways of making people disappear in *Scenes from Family Life* and they always found that the simplest solution was the best.)

Although they can be produced on a minimal budget, I hope the plays challenge young people linguistically. When you read these plays, try to see how each of them uses language. The characters express themselves with different vocabularies, speech patterns and sentence lengths in each of the plays. This might take a bit of working on when you stage the plays.

Totally Over You is set in our modern celebrity-obsessed world but it takes the form of a classical comedy. Because of this, the characters in the play express themselves in sentences that are longer and more structured than we often use in modern life. Working out how to say these lines so that in performance you have enough breath to say them loud enough and fast enough and still make them sound light and easy will take time. Don't worry if the first time you read them aloud they seem difficult to say: they are written in such a way that it takes rehearsal to get them right.

Even in *Citizenship*, where the language looks most like 'real life', you will need to work out where to breathe, which words to stress, where to speak fast or slow and where to pause. This should be part of your rehearsal process.

Lastly, none of these plays would have existed if it weren't for Suzy Graham-Adriani. She commissioned all three of them and provided staunch inspiration, support and friendship during the writing and production process. She is a significant figure in the production of work for young people and I hope she continues to bring together writers and young actors and audiences for many years to come.

Mark Ravenhill
May 2010

Citizenship

Citizenship was developed by the NT Shell Connections 2005 programme and premiered in the Cottesloe auditorium of the National Theatre, London, in March 2006. The cast was as follows:

Amy	Claire-Louise Cordwell
Tom	Sid Mitchell
Gary	Matt Smith
Ray	Robert Boulter
Stephen	Andrew Garfield
Kerry	Farzana Dua Elahe
Chantel	Andrea Riseborough
Alicia	Naomi Bentley
De Clerk	Richard Dempsey
Melissa	Matti Houghton
Tarot Reader	Joy Richardson
Baby	Alex Tregear
Martin	Javone Prince
Directed by	Anna Mackmin
Designed by	Jonathan Fensom
Lighting by	Jason Taylor
Music by	Paddy Cunneen
Sound Designer	Christopher Shutt

One

Amy, Tom.

Amy   You got the Nurofen?

Tom   Yeah.

Amy   Take four.

Tom   It says two.

Amy   Yeah, but if you're gonna really numb yourself you gotta do four.

Tom   I dunno.

Amy   Do you want it to hurt?

Tom   No.

Amy   Then take four. Here.

Amy *passes* **Tom** *vodka. He uses it to wash down four Nurofen.*

Amy   Now put the ice cube on your ear.

Tom *does this.*

Amy   Now you gotta hold it there till you can't feel nothing.

Tom   Thanks for helping

Amy   It's gonna look good.

Tom   Yeah?

Amy   Yeah, really suit you.

Tom   Thass good.

Amy   You got a nice face.

Tom   I don't like my face.

Amy   I think it's nice.

Tom   Sometimes I look in the mirror and I wish I was dead.

Amy   I got rid of mirrors.

Tom   Yeah.

Amy   Mum read this feng shui thing and it said I wasn't supposed to have them. You numb now?

Tom   Almost. You got a nice face.

Amy   You don't have to lie.

Tom   I'm not. You're fit.

Amy   I know I'm plain. But that's okay. I talked to my therapist.

Tom   What did she say?

Amy   That I have to love myself in case nobody else does.

Tom   Your mum loves you.

Amy   I suppose. You ready now?

Tom   I reckon.

Amy *produces a needle.*

Tom   Is that clean?

Amy   I put it in Dettol.

Tom   Alright.

Amy   Let's start.

She starts to push the needle into **Tom***'s ear but he pulls away.*

Amy   I can't do it if you do that.

Tom   I know.

Amy   You gotta sit still.

Tom   Maybe we should leave it. Maybe not today.

Amy   I thought you wanted an earring.

Tom   I know.

Amy   Thass what you been saying for weeks: I wanna earring, I wanna earring.

Tom   I know, only –

Amy   I'll go careful. Come here. You're a baby.

Tom   No.

Amy   I'll treat you nice and soft. Like a baby.

Tom   Alright.

He comes back.

Amy   Bit more vodka.

Tom *drinks.*

Amy   Bit more.

Tom *drinks.*

Amy   Bit more.

Tom *drinks.* **Amy** *pushes the needle into his ear.*

Tom   Aaaggghhh.

Amy   Thass it.

Tom   It hurts.

Amy   Nearly there.

Tom   Do it quickly. Do it. Aaaggghhh.

Amy   Soon be finished.

Tom   Right. Right. Is there blood?

Amy   What?

Tom   Is there blood?

Amy   I dunno.

Tom   I can feel blood

Amy   Maybe a bit.

Tom   Shit. Shit. Shit.

Amy   It's not much. You're gonna be alright.

Tom   Yeah. Yeah. Yeah. Yeah. Yeah. Yeah. Yeah.

He faints.

Amy   Tom? Tom! Shit. Shit.

She drinks a lot of vodka.

Tom – please.

Her mobile rings.

(*On phone.*) Kez? No. I'm fucking – I'm having a panic attack. Like I used to, yeah. Tom's dead. He's died. Just now. Shit. I killed him. I've killed Tom. I wanna kill myself. Shit.

Tom *groans.*

Amy (*on phone*)   He made a noise. Yeah, well. He came back to life. I gotta go. Kez – I'm going now.

Tom   Whass going on?

Amy   You sort of went.

Tom   Who's on the phone?

Amy   Thass Kerry. She's getting stressed out cos she's gotta give the baby back tomorrow.

Tom   Baby?

Amy   Life Skills.

Tom   Oh yeah.

Amy   You remember Life Skills? Each of the girls has gotta take it in turns to look after this baby – plastic baby. It puts you off having a real one. You could have memory loss.

Tom   No.

Amy   Like Shareen after the overdose. Her mum and dad went to see her in the hospital and she didn't know who they were.

Tom   I haven't got memory loss.

Amy   Alright.

Tom   Fucking stupid idea letting you do that. I should have gone to a fucking professional. Fucking go to somebody who knows what they're fucking doing 'stead of letting you fucking fuck the whole thing up.

Amy   I was trying to help.

Tom   Yeah, well, you're no help – you're rubbish. You're total rubbish.

Amy   Don't give me negative messages.

Tom   Trying to kill me with your stupid needle.

Amy   I can't be around people who give me negative messages.

Tom   I fucking hate you.

Amy   No. I'm sorry. I'm sorry. I'm sorry.

She cries.

Tom   Come on. Don't. No. No.

Amy   I can't do anything right. I'm useless.

Tom   No.

Amy   I am. Thass why I cut myself. Cos I'm totally useless. Ughhh.

Tom   Hey hey hey.

He holds **Amy**.

Tom   Come on. Alright. Alright. Alright. You better?

Amy   I dunno.

Tom   You're alright. You're a good person. I like you.

Amy   Yeah?

Tom   I really like you.

Amy   Thass good.

Tom   You got a nice face.

Amy *kisses* **Tom.**

Tom   Oh.

Amy   Was that wrong?

Tom   I didn't mean you to do that.

Amy   Oh. Right. Right.

Tom   I didn't wanna kiss you. Only –

Amy   Yeah?

Tom   I'm not ready for . . .

Amy   You're fifteen.

Tom   I know.

Amy   You gotta have done . . .

Tom   No.

Amy   Why?

Tom   It doesn't matter.

Amy   Tell me.

Tom   I have this dream. And in this dream I'm kissing someone. Real kissing. Tongues and that. But I can't see who I'm kissing. I don't know if it's a woman. Or a man. I try to see the face. But I can't.

Amy   Are you gay?

Tom   I don't know.

Amy   There's bisexuals.

Tom   You won't tell anyone?

Amy   No. Are you going to decide?

Tom   What?

Amy   What you are?

Tom I don't know.

Amy Or find out?

Tom I don't know.

Amy Don't waste yourself, Tom. You've got a nice face.

Tom Yeah.

Amy *gets a text message.*

Amy It's Kerry. She says the baby's gone to sleep.

Tom It's not real.

Amy It is to her.

Tom I'm gonna go.

Amy Finish off the vodka.

Tom No. Thanks. Forget what I told you.

Amy You're still bleeding. There's still some –

Tom I got coursework.

Exit **Tom**. **Amy** *drinks.*

Two

Gary, **Tom**. *They are smoking a joint.*

Tom Good draw.

Gary Got it off my mum's boyfriend for my birthday. Ten big fat ones for my fifteenth.

Tom Thass cool.

Gary Thass the last. He had a fight with his dealer last night. Dealer come round the house and they had a big barney. An' me mum's ragga CDs got smashed in the ruck.

Tom Shit.

Gary   Yeah. She is well gutted.

Enter **Ray** *and* **Stephen**.

Ray   Wass 'appening?

Gary   Chilling.

Ray   You shag Amy last night? We wanna know. You get jiggy?

Stephen   Jiggy-jiggy.

Ray   Is she your bitch? You ride her like your bitch?

Tom   Fuck's sake.

Gary   You got problems.

Ray   What?

Gary   I'm saying: you got problems.

Ray   What you saying? I got problems.

Gary   Yeah, you got problems. No respec'.

Ray   I respec'.

Gary   No respec' for woman.

Ray   I respec' woman.

Gary   Ride her like a bitch? Didn't he say?

Tom   Yeah.

Ray   That's what I said.

Stephen   He said it.

Ray   That's what I said. I ride her *and* respec' woman.

Stephen   Yeah. Ride and respec'.

Ray   You chat shit. What are you? What is he?

Stephen   He is gay.

Gary   All I'm saying –

Ray   So gay. You are so totally gay, Gary.

Gary   Just sayin' –

Ray   You are like the most totally gay person anyone knows.

Gary   I'm not.

Ray   Gay Gary. Thass what you are. Respec'? What are you chattin'? You're chattin' gay. You are fucking wrong, man. Wrong in your head. Wrong in your, your . . . hormones, man. Totally totally wrong.

Gary   Thass not right.

Ray (*to* **Tom**)   Come on, man. Say something. Tell him.

Tom   I . . .

Ray   You're always watching. You're never talking. Tell him.

Tom   Listen, I wanna –

Ray   You fucking tell him.

Stephen   Tell the battyboy.

Ray   You fucking tell him.

Tom   . . . You're gay, Gary.

Gary   Shit.

Tom   Everyone says it. Everyone calls you it. Gay Gary.

Gary   I know what they say.

Tom   You shouldn't talk gay.

Stephen   Thass right.

Tom   Cos no one likes a person who talks gay.

Gary   You chat shit, Tom.

Ray   Listen, he's tellin' you –

Gary   Same as them. All of you. Chattin' shit. All day long. Mouths moving but it's just: chat, chat, chat. Shit, shit, shit.

Tom   No, no.

Gary   Yeah, yeah.

Tom   No.

Gary   Yeah.

Ray   Fight fight fight.

Stephen   Fight fight fight.

Ray   Fight fight fight.

Stephen   Fight.

Tom *pushes* **Gary**.

Ray   Thass it.

Stephen   Do it back or you're gay.

Gary   Fuck's sake.

Gary *pushes* **Tom**.

Ray   Fucking insulted you, man. The gay boy insulted you.

Stephen   Batty hit yer.

Ray   Get him.

Tom   Listen –

Ray   Use your fist.

Stephen   Fist for the battyboy.

Gary   Go on.

Tom   Yeah?

Gary   Do what they tell you. Do what they want to.

Tom   Yeah?

Gary   Follow the leader.

Tom　Yeah.

Tom *punches* **Gary** *in the stomach.*

Ray　Respec', man.

Stephen　Total respec'.

Gary　Fuck you.

Gary *punches* **Tom** *in the stomach very hard.* **Tom** *falls over.*

Ray　Nasty.

Enter **Amy**, **Kerry**, **Alicia**, **Chantal**. **Chantal** *carries the baby.*

Kerry　You're not carrying her properly.

Chantal　Leave it, Kez.

Kerry　But you're not doing the head right.

Chantal　It's my baby, Kez.

Kerry　I know.

Chantal　Yesterday it was yours and now it's mine.

Kerry　I'm only telling you.

Chantal　An' I can do whatever I want with it.

Amy　She's got withdrawal symptoms.

Chantal　Over plastic?

Kerry　Don't say that. You're not fit.

Alicia　Iss the Blazin' Squad. You mellowin'?

Ray　Totally chilled, me darlin'.

Stephen　Totally.

Alicia　Sweet.

Ray　Hear Tom was round yours last night.

Amy　Thass right.

Ray　Gettin' jiggy.

Amy   Do what?

Ray   Jiggy-jiggy-jiggy.

Stephen   Jiggy-jiggy-jiggy.

Amy   You say that?

Tom   No.

Ray   What? You never?

Amy   Thass right.

Ray   What? He not fit enough for you?

Amy   Iss not that.

Ray   You frigid? She frigid, Tom?

Tom   No.

Ray   Wass wrong with 'em? Why ain't they gettin' jiggy?

Alicia   I dunno.

Ray   Thass gay.

Tom   What?

Ray   Youse two are so gay.

Tom/Amy   No.

Ray   Oooo – sore.

Amy   Your ear's started.

Tom   Yeah?

Amy   You started bleeding again.

Alicia   Shit. There's blood.

Kerry   I don't wanna look.

Amy   You wanna look after that. You got a hanky?

Tom   No.

Amy   Chantal?

Chantal   Here.

Chantal *tucks the baby under her arm to find a paper hanky.*

Kerry   You can't do that.

Chantal   Juss for a moment.

Kerry   You got to hold it properly all day long.

Chantal   Juss while I'm lookin'.

Kerry   Give it me. Give it me.

Kerry *takes the baby from* **Chantal**. **Chantal** *finds the hanky, passes it to* **Amy**. **Amy** *holds the hanky on* **Tom**'s *ear.*

Kerry (*to baby*)   Alright. Alright.

Amy   You wanna hold that there?

Ray   She bite you?

Stephen   Yeah.

Ray   While you were doing it?

Tom   It'll be alright now.

Amy   You sure?

Tom   Yeah.

Tom *continues to hold the handkerchief on his ear.*

Chantal   Give me the baby, Kerry.

Kerry   Later.

Chantal   Now.

Kerry   Bit longer.

Chantal   I gotta have it for Life Skills.

Kerry   I know.

Chantal   So . . . ?

Alicia   Give it, Kez.

Kerry Juss . . . do the head properly.

Chantal Alright.

Kerry *hands* **Chantal** *the baby.*

Alicia Thass it. Come on.

Exit **Alicia, Kerry, Chantal.**

Amy Laters.

Exit **Amy.**

Ray How do you do the ear? She do that ear? Was she like eatin' you?

Tom Won't stop bleeding.

Ray What do you do?

Tom It was . . . we were doing an earring?

Ray Earring? Earring? Earring? Shit man. In that ear? You was doing an earring in that ear? Shit, man. Thass the gay side. Shit. You was doing an earring in the gay side. Shit.

Stephen Shit.

Tom No. No. I'm jokin'. It was –

Ray Yeah? Yeah?

Tom It wasn't –

Ray Yeah? Yeah?

Tom It was bitin'.

Ray Yeah?

Stephen Yeah?

Tom It was like love-biting.

Ray I knew it.

Stephen Thass right.

Tom We were gettin' hot and biting and that and we –

Ray Yeah?

Tom And we got –

Stephen Jiggy.

Tom Yeah. Jiggy.

Ray I knew it.

Tom Yeah, totally jiggy. Like ridin' and ridin' and ridin'.

Ray Oh yeah.

Tom And she was wantin' it.

Stephen Yeah.

Tom And I was givin' like, like, like, like –

Ray Yeah.

Tom A big man.

Ray Thass right. Big man.

Stephen Big man.

Ray Big man.

Stephen Big man.

Ray Big man.

Stephen Big man.

Gary Hey – that's sweet.

Ray Shut it, gay boy.

Stephen The big man is talkin', battyboy.

Ray Out of ten?

Tom She's a six.

Ray So you see her again?

Tom Maybe. I'm thinkin' about it.

Stephen De Clerk.

Ray   Run.

Gary   Give us a hand.

Ray   On your own, man.

Ray *and* **Stephen** *exit rapidly.* **Tom** *goes to help* **Gary**. *Enter* **De Clerk**.

De Clerk   Tom.

Tom   Sir?

De Clerk   A word – now. Gary – move.

Gary   Sir.

De Clerk   You're a stoner, Gary.

Gary   The herb is the people's weed.

De Clerk   Piss off.

Exit **Gary**. **De Clerk** *pulls out a piece of coursework.*

De Clerk   What's this, Tom?

Tom   My Citizenship, sir.

De Clerk   Your Citizenship coursework. And what's this?

Tom   Blood, sir.

De Clerk   Blood on your Citizenship coursework. Blood on the work which tomorrow inspectors are going to want to see.

Tom   I know, sir.

De Clerk   And it's not going to be you that's going to be bollocked, is it? No. It's going to be me. Didn't I say, didn't I say many, many – oh so many – times that your coursework should be neat?

Tom   Yes, sir.

De Clerk   Because I don't need the hassle from the inspectors. Because I'm very stressed out. I'm not sleeping. I told you all that I wasn't sleeping. Some nights nothing. Some nights just a couple of hours.

Tom   I know, sir.

De Clerk   The Head gives me grief, kids give me grief. And now tomorrow the inspection team arrives and what do I find?

Tom   I'm sorry, sir.

De Clerk   I find that you have been bleeding all over 'What Does a Multicultural Society Mean to Me?'.

Tom   I didn't mean to.

De Clerk   I'm not showing this to the inspectors. You can stay behind tonight and copy this out.

Tom   But sir –

De Clerk   You want me to copy it out? I've got lesson plans, marking. I'm going to be here till midnight. I'm not copying it out. You'll see me at the end of school and you'll copy this out.

Tom   Yes, sir.

De Clerk   Right then. See you tonight.

Exit **De Clerk**. **Tom** *mops his ear. The bleeding has stopped. Enter* **Amy**.

Amy   Why you tell 'em you slept with me?

Tom   I never.

Amy   Don't lie. You tole Ray and Steve. Now they tole everyone.

Tom   I'm sorry.

Amy   But it's not true.

Tom   I know.

Amy   So why you – ? You gotta sort out what you are, Tom. You straight? You gay?

Tom   Don't say it in school.

Amy   You bisexual? If you want you can see my therapist. My mum'll sort it out.

Tom   I don't need a therapist.

Amy   I know somewhere they do tarot. The card might tell you.

Tom   I don't believe in that.

Amy   What you gonna do, Tom? You gotta stop lying. You gotta decide what you are.

Tom   I know.

Three

Tom *and* **De Clerk**. **Tom** *holds a bloody handkerchief to his ear.*

Tom   I'm still bleeding, sir.

De Clerk   Just – copy it out.

Tom   I am. I'm just . . . worried.

De Clerk   Mmmmmm.

Tom   You know – worried that I might copy it but then I might drip blood on the, like, copy, you know.

De Clerk   Well, don't.

Tom   I'm trying, only –

De Clerk   Put the paper over there, lean your head over there.

Tom   Alright. (*Does this.*) It feels really weird, sir.

De Clerk   Shut up.

Tom   I'm not writing straight, sir.

De Clerk   Do the best you can.

Tom   I'm trying hard but it's not going straight, sir.

De Clerk Fuck's sake, Tom.

Tom Thought so. I just dripped. Blood on the folder.

De Clerk Haven't you got a plaster?

Tom I asked at the front office, but the rules say we have to provide our own.

De Clerk Well, alright – just try not to drip any more.

Tom Doing my best.

De Clerk's *mobile rings.*

Tom You gonna get that, sir?

De Clerk No.

Mobile stops.

Tom Might have been important.

De Clerk Nothing else matters. Nothing else matters but your coursework and the inspectors and that we don't become a failing school, okay? There is nothing else in the whole wide world that matters apart from that.

Mobile rings again.

Tom They don't think so.

De Clerk Well fuck 'em, fuck 'em, fuck 'em.

Tom They really want to talk to you.

De Clerk Uhhh.

He answers the mobile.

No. Still at – I told you. I told you. Because we've got the inspectors. No. No. Well, put it in the fridge and I'll . . . put it in the bin. I don't care. I don't care. I can't.

He ends the call.

Tom Are you married, sir?

De Clerk I'm not talking any more.

Tom   I was just wondering.

De Clerk   Well, don't.

Tom   Other teachers say: my wife this or my girlfriend that. But you never do.

De Clerk   Well, that's up to them.

Tom   It makes you wonder. We all wonder.

De Clerk   Listen, I'm here from eight in the morning until eight in the evening, midnight the last few weeks – maybe I don't have a personal life.

Tom   Yeah.

De Clerk   Maybe I'm not a person at all. Maybe I'm just lesson plans and marking.

Tom   Yeah. Maybe.

De Clerk   Oh. My head. Have you got a Nurofen?

Tom   Sorry, sir?

De Clerk   Have you got a Nurofen or something?

Tom   No, sir. I had some but I took them all.

De Clerk   Right.

Tom   If you want to go home – go home to your . . . partner.

De Clerk   I can't.

Tom   I can do a massage, sir. I know how to do a massage.

De Clerk   No.

Tom   It stops headaches. I done it loads of times.

De Clerk   Listen. Physical contact is –

Tom   Out of lessons now.

De Clerk   Difficult.

Tom   Shhhhhh. Our secret.

He moves over to **De Clerk** *and massages his shoulders and neck.*

Tom   You've got to breathe too. Remember to keep breathing.

De Clerk   Mmmmm.

Tom   There's a lot of stress about, isn't there?

De Clerk   It's all stress.

Tom   How old are you?

De Clerk   Twenty-two.

Tom   Lots of teachers burn out before they're twenty-five because of all the stress.

De Clerk   Mmmmm.

Tom   You're quite developed, sir. Do you go to the gym?

De Clerk   Sometimes.

Tom   With your . . . partner.

De Clerk   Back to your work now. That was wrong. Physical contact.

Tom   Sir – I'm really sorry, but I've –

Tom *wipes* **De Clerk***'s shoulder.*

Tom   I've dripped on you, sir.

De Clerk   What?

Tom   You've got blood on your shirt.

De Clerk   Oh fuck.

Tom   I'm really sorry. It's a really nice shirt.

De Clerk   Shit. Shit. Shit.

He scrubs at his shoulder.

Tom   If you want me to get you another one, sir –

De Clerk   No no.

Tom   I get a discount. My brother manages Top Man.

De Clerk   Tom – get on with your work. You get on with your work and I'll get on with my work.

Tom   You've got good clothes, sir. For a teacher.

De Clerk   Tom.

Pause.

Tom   Sir . . . I keep on having this dream and in this dream I'm being kissed.

De Clerk   Don't.

Tom   Only I never know whether it's a man or woman who's doing the kissing.

De Clerk   This isn't Biology. I'm Citizenship.

Tom   I think I dream about being kissed by a man.

De Clerk   I don't want to know about that.

Tom   I really want to know: so I dream about a man kissing me?

De Clerk   Please. Don't do this. I'm tired. I'm exhausted. I've got the Head of Department chasing me. I've got the inspectors coming after me like wolves after blood. I've still got eight hours of paperwork. And I've done a full day's teaching. Please understand the pressure I'm under and just copy the work.

Tom   What do you do if you're gay, sir?

De Clerk   You talk to someone.

Tom   I'm trying to talk to you.

De Clerk   You don't talk to me. Talk to your form tutor.

Tom   He hates me.

De Clerk   I don't think so.

Tom What do you do at the weekends, sir?

De Clerk Alright. Go away. Go home.

Tom What about the coursework?

De Clerk I'll explain the blood to the inspectors.

Tom Alright then.

He packs up his bag.

Bye then, sir.

De Clerk Bye, Tom.

Tom I want to talk to someone gay, sir. I don't know any.

De Clerk Shut up, please shut up.

Tom I really want to meet someone gay and ask them what it's like.

De Clerk Well – it's fine. It's normal. It's just fine.

Tom You reckon?

De Clerk You know the school policy: we celebrate difference. You report bullies. Everything's okay. You're okay.

Tom I don't feel okay.

De Clerk Well – you should do.

Four

Gary, Tom. *Smoking a joint.*

Gary Was it good?

Tom What?

Gary You know – when you done Amy?

Tom Well . . .

Gary Cos lovin'. There's so many types of lovin'.

Tom   Yeah?

Gary   Yeah. Between man and woman. There's so many types of lovin', in't there?

Tom   You reckon?

Gary   Oh yeah. There's sweet lovin' and there's animal lovin' and there's hard lovin' and there's dirty lovin'. There's millions of ways of lovin'. You follow?

Tom   I think so.

Gary   You lie.

Tom   No.

Gary   I'm chattin' shit, aren't I?

Tom   No.

Gary   Yeah, I'm chattin' shit. Thass the herb. I always chat shit when I'm blazin'. But thass the way I like it. I like to chat shit.

Tom   I like the way you talk.

Gary   Yeah?

Tom   You talk good. You're better than the knobheads. Ray, Steve – they're knobheads.

Gary   Then how come you –

Tom   Yeah yeah.

Gary   – hit me when they tell you?

Tom   I'm sorry.

Gary   No worries. Love and understanding. Peace to you, brother.

Tom   Yeah, peace.

Gary   To mellow, man. Love you, brother.

Tom   Yeah. Brother love.

Gary *puts his arm round* **Tom.**

Gary   You like the brother love?

Tom   Yeah, it's good.

Gary   Peace on the planet. No war. Herb bring harmony. Blaze some more?

Tom   Yeah.

Gary *produces another rolled joint from a tin.*

Gary   So tell me 'bout your lovin'?

Tom   Well –

Gary   Is she your woman now?

Tom   Well –

Gary   Or was it like a one-night lovin' ting?

Tom   Well –

Gary   Don't be shy. Take a big draw and tell.

He hands **Tom** *the joint.* **Tom** *draws.*

Gary   Harder, man. Draw as deep as you can.

Tom *draws as hard as he can.*

Tom   I need some water.

Gary   No. Not till you tell. Tell me what it was like. Come on, man.

Tom   I feel ill.

Gary   I gotta know. I gotta know about the ride.

Gary *pins* **Tom** *to the floor, knees over his arms, sitting on his chest.*

Gary   What was it like when you rode the woman?

Tom   Get off me – off me.

Gary   Jiggy-jiggy with the honey. Ya!

Tom   Off.

He pushes **Gary** *off.*

Tom   I never, alright? I never –

Gary   What?

Tom   I never done her. We never done anything.

Gary   What? Nothing? Oral? Finger?

Tom   Nothing, okay. We never done it.

Gary   Shit. You lied.

Tom   Yeah.

Gary   That's sad, man.

Tom   Yeah, it's really sad.

Gary   So – you not gonna tell me 'bout no lovin'?

Tom   No.

Gary   Shit, broth'. That was gonna be my wank tonight.

Tom   Yeah?

Gary   Yeah – your booty grindin' her. That was gonna –

Tom   Well, there's nothing.

Gary   You wanna pretend for me? Like make it up. So – you never done it. But you can make up like a story, like a dirty story so I got summat in my head.

Tom   I'm not good at stories.

Gary   Just make it dirty so I got something for tonight.

Tom   I'm still supposed to copy out my Citizenship for De Clerk.

Gary   Okay – tell me about your dreams. You gotta have dirty dreams.

Tom   Course.

Gary Then tell me –

Tom I don't know.

Gary Come, brother love. (*Sits* **Tom** *down, puts his arms around him.*) Tell your brother.

Tom . . . I have this dream. And in this dream I'm lying in bed. Not in my room. Not like my room at home. Like a strange room.

Gary Like a dungeon?

Tom No, maybe like a Travel Lodge or something, I don't know.

Gary Right.

Tom And I'm almost asleep but then the door opens and this stranger comes into the room.

Gary Like a thief?

Tom Maybe but this . . . person, they come over to the bed and they kiss me.

Gary Right. And – ?

Tom It's a person but I don't know, I don't know –

Gary Yeah.

Tom See, this person, are they a woman or are they . . . ?

Gary Yeah?

Tom *leans over and kisses* **Gary** *on the lips.*

Gary You're battyman?

Tom I don't know.

Gary Shit, blud, you're battyman. The battyman kissed me. Shit.

Gary *moves away and takes several draws.*

Tom   I don't know. Don't know. Just wanted to see, you know
– just wanted to see what it felt like if I –

Gary   And did you like it?

Tom   I don't know.

Gary   Was my lips sweet?

Tom   I don't know.

Gary   No, blud, thass cool, thass cool, I can handle that.
Peace to all. Everybody's different. I can go with that.

Tom   I'm sorry.

Gary   Hey – love you still, bro'.

He hugs **Tom**.

Tom   I just thought – you're Gay Gary.

Gary   Thass just a name. You touch my arse I kill you, see?

Tom   Okay.

Gary   No, see, I like the honeys. You should see my site.
Thass where I live out what's in my head, see?

He gets out his laptop, opens his website.

See, these are my fantasies. And I share him with the world on
my message board. I got graphics, see?

Tom   Is that you?

Gary   Yeah.

Tom   You got muscles.

Gary   Yeah, well – thass me older, see. And thass my dick.

Tom (*laughs*)   I thought it was a weapon.

Gary (*laughs*)   Yeah. My dick's a lethal weapon. And I fight
my way through the desert, see, through all the terrorists and
that, see? Nuke nuke nuke. And then when I get to the city –
there's all the honeys, see? And I ride 'em, see. And then I kill
'em.

Tom   That's sick, man. I thought you was all love and understanding.

Gary   Can't help what's in my head. Gotta let it out.

Tom   All that – it's . . . wrong.

Gary   Stuff that's in my head. I don't fight it. I let it out. Thass your problem. What's in your head, Tom? Who do you want? The honey or the homo?

Tom   I dunno yct. I want to find out. I gotta try different stuff.

Gary   You wanna get online.

Tom   You reckon?

Gary   Yeah. You start searchin', chatting, message boards, stuff. You can try everything.

Tom   Yeah?

Gary   You wanna do a search now? 'Gay sex'? 'Battyman'?

Tom   No.

Gary   What you want?

Tom   I don't know. Maybe I'll do Amy.

Gary   You reckon?

Tom   I could do if I wanted to, yeah.

Five

Tom *and* **Amy**. **Tom** *carries hair dye.* **Amy** *has a bandage round her wrist.*

Tom   See? It's baby blonde.

Amy   Right.

Tom   I wanna go baby blonde.

Amy   Right.

Tom   And I want you to do it to me.

Amy   I'm supposed to be doing my affirmations.

Tom   What's that?

Amy   I'm supposed to write out a hundred times 'I'm surrounded by love'.

Tom   Why?

Amy   Cos I cut myself again last night.

Tom   Why?

Amy   I dunno. I was bored. Or something. Or stress. I dunno.

Tom   You gotta know.

Amy   I don't. Mum took me down the healer and she told me I had to do the affirmations.

Tom   You can do them later. Do my hair.

Amy   They don't work anyway.

Tom   No?

Amy   I did them before and they never worked.

Tom   What works?

Amy   I dunno. Melissa says I need a shag.

Tom   Maybe you do.

Amy   You reckon?

Tom   Yeah. I reckon.

Amy   There's no one fancies me.

Tom   That's not true.

Amy   Says who?

Tom   Says me.

Amy   Yeah?

Tom   You gonna do my hair?

Amy   If you want.

Tom   We need a bowl of water.

Amy   Alright.

Tom   And a towel.

Amy   Yeah yeah.

Tom   Thanks.

Amy *exits.* **Tom** *removes his shirt. Folds it up. Arranges himself on the floor. Pause. Enter* **Melissa.**

Melissa   Alright?

Tom   Alright.

Melissa   You seen my iPod?

Tom   No.

Melissa   She takes my iPod. Drives me mental. We're always having words. There'll be a ruck soon.

Tom   Right.

Melissa   You shagging?

Tom   Not yet.

Melissa   Do us all a favour and give her one, will you?

Tom   Do my best.

Melissa   Where the fuck's it gone?

Exit **Melissa. Tom** *arranges himself again on the floor to look as alluring and yet as natural as possible for* **Amy.** *Enter* **Amy** *with bowl of water and towel.*

Amy   I got it.

Tom   I took my top off.

Amy   Right.

Tom   Cos I don't want to get bleach on it.

Amy   Right.

Tom   That alright? Me getting naked?

Amy   Whatever. You got the instructions?

Tom   Yeah.

He gives **Amy** *the instructions.*

Tom   I've been thinking about what you said.

Amy (*reading instructions*)   Yeah?

Tom   About sorting myself out and that. In my head. You know – about whether I wanted . . . you.

Amy   You seen a therapist?

Tom   No. I just been thinking.

Amy   Right.

Tom   About who I wanna kiss and that.

Amy   Right. You got any allergies?

Tom   Why?

Amy   Cos it says here – (*the instructions*) You got any allergies?

Tom   Dust and peanuts.

Amy   Dust and peanuts should be alright. You wanna get started?

Tom   If you like. What if you got bleach on your top?

Amy   It's a crap top.

Tom   Yeah, but you'd ruin it. Bleach down the front.

Amy   Mum'll recycle it.

Tom   Maybe you better take your top off too.

Amy   I don't think so.

Tom   Go on. I took my top off. Time you took your top off too.

Amy   No.

Tom   Come on. Take it off. Take it off.

Tom *reaches out to* **Amy** *– she pushes him away.*

Amy   I'm not taking my top off, alright?

Tom   Alright. Do you reckon I should go down the gym?

Amy   I don't know.

Tom   Maybe I should go down the gym. My body's stupid.

Amy   No.

Tom   I've got a stupid body.

Amy   No. You've got a fit body. I like your body.

Tom   Yeah?

Amy   It's a nice body.

Tom   Do you wanna touch it?

Amy   I dunno.

Tom   Come on. Touch it if you like.

Amy   Alright.

Amy *reaches out to touch* **Tom.** *Enter* **Melissa** *followed by* **Chantal, Kerry** *and* **Alicia. Alicia** *carries the baby.*

Melissa   Your mates are here. They're shagging.

Exit **Melissa.**

Chantal/Kerry/Alicia   Alright?

Tom   Alright.

Amy   We're not – we weren't gonna –

Chantal   Thass a buff bod.

Tom   Yeah?

Chantal   For a kid, you're fit. He's fit, isn't he?

Kerry   He's alright. I mean I wouldn't –

Amy   We weren't gonna –

Kerry   But yeah, he's alright.

Amy   I was gonna dye his hair.

Chantal   Go on then.

Tom   Forget it.

Chantal   No. Go on.

Tom   Another time. I don't want people watching.

Chantal   It's safe. Go on. We heard you cut yourself again. You alright?

Amy   Oh yeah. I'm fine. Come on – let's wash your hair.

Amy *pours water over* **Tom***'s head.*

Tom   Owww! Hurts! Awwww! Burning, aagh!

Amy   Shit.

Tom   What you – ? You put cold in that? You never put any cold in that.

Amy   I forgot.

Tom   You forgot. Shit. I'm gonna be scarred. Ugh.

Amy   I'll get cold.

She runs out with the jug. **Tom** *paces around scratching at his scalp, groaning.* **Alicia** *get out cigarettes.*

Kerry   Lish – don't.

Alicia   What?

Kerry   Not around the kid.

Alicia   Don't be stupid.

Kerry   It stunts 'em.

Alicia   Thass when you're pregnant.

Kerry   Not when you're mother.

She takes the packet of cigarettes from **Alicia**.

Alicia   Fuck's sake. I get stressed out without 'em.

Kerry   Yeah – well.

Alicia   See that, Spazz? Took my fags.

Kerry   Don't call it that.

Alicia   Whatever.

Enter **Amy** *with jug of cold water.*

Amy   Here.

Tom *kneels in front of bowl.* **Amy** *pours cold water over his head.*

Tom   Aaaggghhh.

He lies back.

Amy   You better now.

Tom   Is there red? Like burns?

Amy   A bit.

Tom   Thought so.

Chantal   Are you gonna shag? Cos we can leave if you're gonna shag.

Tom   No. We're not gonna shag.

Chantal   You sure?

Tom   Yeah. I'm sure. We're not gonna shag. We're never gonna . . . no.

Six

Tom, Tarot Reader. *Nine cards spread out in a fan – three lines of three.*

Tarot Reader   There's the tower. You see? That's the tower. Now – you are facing a moment of great change. A moment of great decision. Would you like to ask me a question?

Tom   I . . . no.

Tarot Reader   Any moment you need to – you must ask me a question.

Tom   Alright.

Tarot Reader   But the tower makes sense to you?

Tom   Yes.

Tarot Reader   The foundation on which – you see here these are your emotions – the foundations on which your emotions are based is unstable. It may collapse at any time.

Tom   Yes. That's how I feel.

Tarot Reader   Then the cards are speaking to you?

Tom   Yes, yes, they are.

Tarot Reader   Good. Good.

Tom   Nothing feels . . . fixed. Everything feels as though it could fall over. I'm confused.

Tarot Reader   Lots of people –

Tom   I don't know who I am. I want to know –

Tarot Reader   That's how lots of people –

Tom   I need to know. I need to choose.

Tarot Reader   Of course, yes yes, but please . . . listen . . . so many people are . . . Nobody knows . . . All the time we're told choose, decide . . .

Tom   Yes.

Tarot Reader   All the time, we've got these choices.

Tom   I know.

Tarot Reader   And we feel so unprepared, but if we explore the choices, if we tune our hearts and our heads to the cards. Do you see? Do you see?

Tom   I think so.

Tarot Reader   Good. Good. Let's look at the future.

Tom   Yes.

Tarot Reader   Now this is – the cards are very strong here.

Tom   That's good.

Tarot Reader   Two of the major . . . we call these the major arcana, you see? Here – the pictures. The High Priestess – here. Drawing back the veil. Drawing back the veil to let you into her world.

Tom   It's a woman?

Tarot Reader   She's a feminine –

Tom   It's a woman letting me into her – I've got to know – that's a woman –

Tarot Reader   It's more complicated than that. Yes, we used to say: the cards are men and they are women. The King. The Queen. But in this day and age – it's more complex – we prefer the masculine and feminine energies.

Tom   But she's a woman.

Tarot Reader   Or a man with a feminine energy.

Tom   Oh.

Tarot Reader   And here – the lovers. You are about to enter the gate, pass the threshold and embrace the lovers. A lover for you. Yes? You've got a question?

Tom I've really got to know. Is it? Is it a . . . a man or a woman?

Tarot Reader It's not so simple. Look at the cards. Really listen to the cards. You are about to pass through the gateway and meet your lover. Man or a woman? What do the cards say?

Tom I can't . . . Nothing.

Tarot Reader Make yourself comfortable. Be patient. Listen.

Tom No. I really can't . . .

Tarot Reader We have time. You will choose a course of action. With the cards you will choose a course of action. Just watch and wait and listen. And listen. Listen. Listen to the cards.

Tom *looks at the cards. Long pause.*

Tarot Reader Yes?

Tom Yes.

Tarot Reader You know what to do?

Tom I know what to do.

Seven

Tom, Amy. **Amy** *carries the baby.*

Tom You got the baby.

Amy She made me. Said I'd have detention for a week.

Tom That's harsh.

Amy Totally harsh. I told her – I'm not fit to be a mother, look at my arms. You can't be a mother when you've got cuts all over your arms.

Tom And what did she say?

Amy   Said it would take me out of myself – think about another life.

Tom   Bit of plastic.

Amy   And now I have to write down all my thoughts and feelings in my baby diary.

Tom   What you written?

Amy   Nothing. Don't feel anything. It doesn't do anything. Just sits there. It's heavy.

Tom   Let me feel.

Amy   Go on then.

Amy *gives* **Tom** *the baby.*

Tom   Yeah. Really heavy.

He drops the baby.

Whoops.

Amy   You did that on purpose.

Tom   Maybe.

Amy   You're trouble.

Tom   That's right. Do you reckon it's damaged?

Amy   Shut up.

Tom *picks up the baby.*

Tom   No – it's fine.

Amy   Don't tell Kerry – she'll go mental.

Tom (*to baby*)   You're alright, aren't you? Aren't you? Yes.

Tom *throws the baby up in the air – lets it fall on the floor.*

Amy   You're mad.

Tom   I'm rubbish at catching. Catch it!

Tom *throws the baby to* **Amy**. *She catches it.*

Amy   I'll be bollocked if it's damaged.

Tom   Throw it to me. Come on.

Amy *throws the baby. He lets it fall to the floor again.*

Tom   Why can't I catch it?

Amy   You're not trying. Give it here.

She goes to pick up the baby. **Tom** *stops her.*

Tom   No – leave it.

Amy   Why?

Tom   Cos I'm here. You can hold the baby later.

Amy   What am I gonna write in my baby diary?

Tom   Make it up.

He takes his shirt off.

Amy   What are you doing?

Tom   I went down the gym. See?

Amy   How many times you been?

Tom   Three.

Amy   I don't think three's gonna make a difference.

Tom   Course it is. Have a feel.

Amy   Yeah?

Tom *flexes a bicep.*

Tom   Feel that.

Amy   Alright.

Amy *feels his bicep.*

Tom   See?

Amy   What?

Tom   It's stronger. Harder.

Amy   You reckon?

Tom   Oh yeah – that's much harder.

Amy   I dunno.

She picks up the baby.

Tom   Do you wanna have sex?

Amy   Maybe.

Tom   I think maybe we should have sex.

Amy   I've never had sex before.

Tom   Neither have I. I've seen it online.

Amy   Yeah?

Tom   Round Gary's.

Amy   Gay Gary's?

Tom   He's not gay.

Amy   Right. Are you gay?

Tom   Come here.

Amy *goes to* **Tom.** *He takes the baby out of her arms and lays it on the floor. They kiss.*

Tom   Did you like that?

Amy   Yeah. Is it me?

Tom   What?

Amy   In your dreams? Is it me you're kissing in your dream?

Tom   No.

Amy   Are you sure? If you can't see the face . . . ?

Tom   Yeah, well. But I can feel it.

Amy   And it's not me?

Tom   It's not you. Does that bother you?

Amy   No.

Tom   Good.

They kiss again.

Melissa (*off*)   Amy.

Amy   What?

Melissa (*off*)   You got my camcorder?

Amy   No.

Melissa (*off*)   You sure? I can't find it anywhere.

Amy   I'm sure.

Melissa (*off*)   If you've taken it again . . .

Amy   I haven't taken it again.

Melissa (*off*)   I'm coming to look.

Amy   No.

Exit **Amy**. **Tom** *waits. Enter* **De Clerk**.

Tom   How did you get in here, sir?

De Clerk   Through the floor.

Tom   What? You just . . . ?

De Clerk   Come through the floor.

Tom   Shit.

De Clerk   Just something I can do. Don't tell the Head. We're not supposed to have special powers.

Tom   Alright. Are you here cos I'm still a bit gay – is that it?

De Clerk   Let's not talk about that.

Tom   I sort of decided I wasn't gonna be gay any more – now you sort of – well, it's a bit gay, isn't it, coming through the floor like that?

De Clerk   Are you going to have sex with her?

Tom   Yeah, I reckon. What – don't you think I should?

De Clerk   We can't tell you yes or no. That's not what we do.

Tom   Why not?

De Clerk   Because you have to make your own choices.

Tom   But why? Everything's so confusing. There's so many choices. I don't feel like a person. I just feel like all these bits floating around. And none of them match up. Like a jigsaw that's never going to be finished. It's doing my head in.

De Clerk   And what would you prefer?

Tom   Someone to tell me what to be.

De Clerk   No one's going to do that.

Tom   I wish they would.

De Clerk   When I was growing up: everyone told you who to be. They told you what to do. What was right and what was wrong. What your future would be.

Tom   I'd like that.

De Clerk   No. It made me very unhappy.

Tom   I'm unhappy – too many choices. You were unhappy – no choices. Everyone's unhappy. Life's shit, isn't it, sir?

De Clerk   That is I would say a distinct possibility.

Tom   Are you still unhappy, sir?

De Clerk   If I stop. If I stop working and rushing – the inspection, the continual assessment – trying to pay the mortgage every month, trying to please the Head, trying to get home before nine every night – then, yes, I'm unhappy. But only when I stop.

Tom   You've got a boyfriend?

De Clerk   I can't talk about that.

Tom   You're gay, sir. I don't mean that in a bad way. I just mean – like you know who you are. And you're gay. I'm going to have sex with her.

De Clerk   If that's what you want.

Tom   So you better get back through the floor. I'm not having you watching us.

De Clerk   I don't want to watch. Use protection.

Tom   I know.

De Clerk   If you're having sex, use protection.

Tom   That's telling me what to do.

De Clerk   It's advice.

Tom   It's telling me what to do. You should tell me more of that.

De Clerk   I can't. Promise me you'll use protection.

Tom   I might do.

De Clerk   Promise.

Tom   Do all gay people come through floors?

De Clerk   Now you're being silly.

Enter **Amy**.

Amy   She's gone now.

Tom   Good. (*To* **De Clerk**.) You going?

De Clerk   Take care.

Exit **De Clerk**.

Tom   Is everyone out?

Amy   Yeah. They're all out. Got the place to ourselves.

Tom   That's good.

Amy   Are you scared?

Tom   A bit. Are you?

Amy   Scared and excited.

Tom   We'll take it slow.

Amy   Yeah. Let's take it really slow. You got anything?

Tom   Like what?

Amy   Like condoms and that?

Tom   No.

Amy   Oh.

Tom   Does that bother you?

Amy   No. Does that bother you?

Tom   No.

Amy   Do you love me?

Tom   I don't know. Maybe later. Is that alright?

Amy   Yeah. That's alright.

Tom   After – we can do my hair. I still want blond hair.

Amy   Alright.

Tom   Turn the light out.

Amy   I want to see you.

Tom   No.

Tom *turns the light off. The* **Baby** *comes forward and speaks to the audience.*

Baby   And so it happened. My mummy and my daddy made me that night. Neither of them enjoyed it very much. But they did it. And that's what they wanted. And that night I started to grow in my mummy's tummy. And by the time she did her GCSEs I was almost ready to come out of her tummy.

I think that night as they lay together in the dark she thought they might spend all their time together from that day on. But

that didn't happen. In fact, once that night was over, they
were sort of shy and embarrassed whenever they saw each
other until – by the time I was born – they weren't speaking to
each other at all. And Mummy says for a few moments – she's
sure there were a few moments that night when he did really,
really love her. And I believe her.

They did talk to each other once more after they left school –
but there's one more bit of the story to show you before we get
to that.

Eight

Tom *and* **Martin. Tom** *has a hat pulled down, completely covering
his hair.*

Tom   You've got a nice place.

Martin (*off*)   Thank you.

Tom   Yeah, really nice. Trendy.

Martin (*off*)   Thank you.

Tom   What do you do?

Martin (*off*)   My job?

Tom   Yeah. Your job.

Martin (*off*)   I'm a systems analyst.

Tom   Right. Right. Is that alright?

Martin (*off*)   I enjoy it.

Tom   And the pay's good?

Martin (*off*)   The pay is ridiculously good.

Tom   Well – that's good.

Martin (*off*)   And you?

Tom   What?

Martin (*off*)   Do you have a job?

Tom   Yes.

Martin (*off*)   What do you do?

Tom   Well, actually, I'm looking.

Martin (*off*)   I see.

Enter **Martin**, *with two bottles of beer. He gives one of the bottles of beer to* **Tom**.

Martin   Cheers.

Tom   Right. Cheers.

Martin   If you want to take off –

Tom   I'm alright.

Martin   Maybe – your hat . . . ?

Tom   No.

Martin   Alright.

Tom   It's just I had a disaster.

Martin   Yes?

Tom   With my hair.

Martin   I see.

Tom   Yeah, this mate tried to dye my hair but it went wrong.

Martin   Right.

Tom   Yeah, tried to dye my hair, but I had a bit of a reaction and it's gone really weird, like ginger bits and green bits and that. Last month. I'm waiting for it to grow out. I look weird so that's why I'm wearing –

Martin   It suits you.

Tom   Yeah?

Martin   The hat. It's a good look.

Tom   Thank you.

Martin   You're a good-looking guy.

Tom   Right.

Martin   Was it your boyfriend?

Tom   What?

Martin   With the hair dye?

Tom   No.

Martin   Have you got a boyfriend?

Tom   No. Have you?

Martin   Yes. Is that alright?

Tom   I suppose. How old are you?

Martin   Twenty-one.

Tom   Right.

Martin   How old are you?

Tom   Eighteen.

Martin   You said nineteen in the chatroom.

Tom   Did I?

Martin   Yes

Tom   Well, I'm eighteen.

Martin   But actually you look younger.

Tom   Really?

Martin   You actually look about sixteen.

Tom   Everyone says I look younger. That's what they said when I was at school.

Martin   Right. Do you want to come through to the bedroom?

Tom   In a minute. Are you happy?

Martin   What?

Tom   You know, in your life and that? Does it make you happy?

Martin   I suppose so.

Tom   With your boyfriend and your job and that?

Martin   I never really think about it.

Tom   You seem happy.

Martin   Then I suppose I am.

Tom   That's good.

Martin   And you?

Tom   What?

Martin   Are you happy?

Tom   I reckon. Yes, I am.

Martin   Well, that's good. Look, we really should get into the bedroom –

Tom   Right.

Martin   My boyfriend's coming back at five and I don't want to –

Tom   Right.

Martin   Sorry to hurry you, but –

Tom   That's alright.

Martin   You can keep your hat on.

Tom   Thanks.

Martin   You're cute.

Tom   Thanks. I've never done this before.

Martin   Chatrooms?

Tom   This. All of it.

Martin   Sex?

Tom   No. I've done sex. Only . . .

Martin   Not with someone so old?

Tom   Not with . . .

Martin   Twenty-two too old for you?

Tom   No. Not with . . . a bloke. I mean, I did it with girls, a girl, but . . .

Martin   Did you like it?

Tom   It was alright.

Martin   If you like that kind of thing.

Tom   Yeah. I'm shaking. Sorry. I feel nervous. Is it gonna hurt?

Martin   Not if we do it right.

Tom   How will we know?

Martin   I don't know. You just have to . . . er . . . suck it and see.

Tom (*laughs*)   You dirty bastard.

Martin   Yeah.

Tom   I shouldn't have come.

Martin   Alright then – another time. How are you getting back?

Tom   No, no.

He kisses **Martin.**

Martin   Mixed messages.

Tom   You're right. I'm sixteen.

Martin   I know.

Tom   I'm legal.

Martin   What do you want?

Tom   This.

He kisses **Martin.**

Tom   Come on then. Where's the bedroom? Or do you want your boyfriend to find out?

Martin   The bedroom's through there.

Tom   Your boyfriend, he's not . . . ?

Martin   Yes?

Tom   He's not . . . is your boyfriend a teacher?

Martin *(laughs)*   God, no. He's a mortgage broker. Why?

Tom   Nothing.

Martin   Ready?

Tom   Ready. Just – don't touch my hat, alright?

Martin   Alright.

Nine

Amy, Tom.

Amy   Your hair's alright.

Tom   Yeah. Took a few months. But in the end it went back to normal.

Amy   You should still do an earring.

Tom   You reckon?

Amy   Yeah. I always reckoned an earring would really suit you.

Tom   Maybe one day.

Amy   Yeah. One day. What you up to?

Tom   Not much. I'm going to college next year.

Amy   That's good.

Tom   Fashion.

Amy   Nice.

Tom   And I'm doing coat-check.

Amy   In a club?

Tom   Sort of pub-club.

Amy   Gay club?

Tom   Just Fridays and Saturdays. You should come along. It's a laugh.

Amy   You got a boyfriend?

Tom   I dunno.

Amy   You got to know.

Tom   There's a bloke . . . We . . . meet up. A couple of times a week. But he's living with someone.

Amy   His boyfriend.

Tom   Yeah. He's got a boyfriend. He keeps on saying they're gonna split but they haven't. Still – we have a laugh. He's got money.

Amy   Right.

Tom   You seeing anyone?

Amy   Yeah.

Tom   Who?

Amy   Nosy. I mean, I can't go out much but, you know, if I get a babysitter –

Tom   Right.

Amy   I'm gonna do college in a couple of years.

Tom   That's good.

Amy   Just gotta wait till she's a bit older.

Tom   Of course. If you need me to babysit –

Amy   No.

Tom   I don't mind.

Amy   I've got mates do that for me. Kerry loves it.

Tom   Yeah, but if you ever need me to –

Amy   I don't need you to.

Tom   I want to.

Amy   I don't want you to, alright?

Tom   Alright. I still . . . think about you.

Amy   Right.

Tom   Like . . . fancy you and that.

Amy   You told your boyfriend?

Tom   Sometimes, when he kisses me, I think about you. He kisses me but I close my eyes and it's your face I see.

Amy   You can't have it both ways.

Tom   That's what I want.

Amy   Well – you can't have it.

Enter **Gary**, *pushing a pram.*

Gary   Alright, babe?

Amy   Yeah. Alright.

Gary *kisses* **Amy**.

Amy   She been alright?

Gary   Yeah. Fast asleep the whole time.

Amy   She'll be awake all night now.

Gary   You want me to wake her?

Amy   No. Leave her alone.

Gary   Alright, Tom?

Tom   She told me she was going out with someone.

Gary   You guess who?

Tom   No. You gonna bring the kid up to be a stoner too?

Gary   No. I give up the weed, didn't I? Can't be blazing around the kid, can I? Once you got a kid to look after – that's the time to grow up, I reckon.

Tom   Yeah – suppose that's right.

Amy   Tom's gone gay now.

Gary   Thass cool.

Tom   Can I have a look at her?

Amy   We gotta go in a minute. Mum's booked us up the naturopath.

Tom   I just want to have a quick look.

Amy   Go on then.

Tom   She's beautiful.

Amy   Yeah. She's alright.

Tom   Can I pick her up?

Amy   No.

Tom   I'll be careful.

Amy   I don't want you to.

Tom   Alright.

Amy   Not now she's settled.

Tom   Alright.

Amy   Best to leave her alone.

Tom   Alright.

Amy   I want to keep her out of the sun.

Tom   Of course.

Gary   We've got to get the bus.

Amy   Yeah.

Tom   Will I see you again?

Amy   Maybe.

Tom   I wanna see you again. I'm the dad.

Amy   Gary looks after her – don't you?

Gary   Yeah.

Tom   Yeah – but still.

Enter **Martin***.*

Martin   Sorry, I tried to get away only –

Martin *goes to kiss* **Tom***. He steps away.*

Tom   Don't.

Amy   You his boyfriend?

Martin   I wouldn't . . . sort of . . .

Tom   Yeah. Only sort of.

Amy   Better than nothing though, isn't it?

Martin   That's right.

Amy   See ya.

Exit **Amy** *and* **Gary** *with pram.*

Tom   Did you tell him?

Martin   What?

Tom   You know. About me. You were supposed to tell him about me.

Martin   He's away this weekend. What do you want to do?

Tom   Do you love me?

Martin   You know I don't like to use that word.

Tom   Because?

Martin   Because.

Tom   Tell me.

Martin   What does it mean? It doesn't mean anything. 'Love'? It doesn't mean . . .

Tom   You've got to say it.

Martin   No.

Tom   There's no point to this. There's no point to anything. What's the point?

Martin   Money. Sex. Fun. That's the point.

Tom   No. I want –

Martin   What?

Tom   Say you love me.

Martin   No.

Tom   Say you love me.

Martin   No.

Tom   Say you love me. Please. Please. Please – say you love me.

Martin   Okay. I love you – okay?

Beat.

Tom   . . . No.

Martin   Fuck's sake. Why can't you . . . moneysexfun?

Tom   Because I want more. I want everything. I want . . .

Martin   Yes?

Tom   I want everything and I want . . . I want . . . I want to find out everything.

Martin (*laughs*)   You're a baby. Treat you like a baby.

Tom   No. Not any more. No.

Scenes from Family Life

Characters

Jack
Lisa
Stacy
Barry

Karen
Holly
Tony
Matt
Marie
Ryan

Soldier 1
Soldier 2
Soldier 3
Mother *with an empty pram*

Parents, Babies, Entertainer

All characters are aged sixteen to eighteen

Setting
Living room of Jack and Lisa's flat

One

Living room of **Jack** *and* **Lisa***'s flat.*

Lisa Feel?

Jack Yeah.

Jack *reaches out and touches* **Lisa***'s stomach.*

Lisa Head and feet and . . . Tiny but somewhere there's . . .

Jack Yeah.

Lisa You thought of names?

Jack Not yet. You?

Lisa A few but . . . Don't want to jinx it.

Jack Too soon.

Lisa Yeah.

Jack What's it feel like?

Lisa Different.

Jack Does it send you messages and stuff? Through your body?

Lisa I dunno. Maybe. Yeah.

Jack You gotta know.

Lisa No.

Jack What's going on in your head?

Lisa Happiness. You. Me. Baby.

Jack That all?

Lisa Yeah.

Jack You sure . . . ?

Lisa I can't tell you every –

Jack But that's what I want to know.

Lisa It's just not possible. You ready to be a dad?

Jack   I am totally, totally ready.

Lisa   My mum she says we're too young but I say Jack's got a job, I got a job, we got the flat, it's time. I love you.

Jack   And I love you.

They kiss.

Together for ever. You feel trapped?

Lisa   No. Love it. Love you.

Jack   Am I boring?

Lisa   Normal.

Jack   I'll get the tea.

Exit **Jack**. *Whoosh, flash,* **Lisa** *vanishes into thin air. Re-enter* **Jack**.

Jack   Lisa do you want white or the . . . ? Lees? Lees? Lisa?

Pause.

Lisa?

Pause.

Lisa!

Pause.

LISA?

He hunts around the room.

I'm gonna find you and when I find you I'm gonna . . . Lisa?

He goes and checks in the bedroom.

(*Off*.) Lisa!

He enters from the bedroom. She reappears – a rematerialisation.

Oh my God. Oh my oh oh –

Lisa   What? What?

Jack I . . . There was nothing there. It was frightening. There was like this gap where a person should be and I was calling out but there was nothing there. And then you were there.

Lisa Stop messing around.

Jack I'm not, I – Oh Lees. You think I'm going mad? Maybe . . .

Lisa Forget it. Trick of the light. Kiss me.

Jack Listen I . . . can't.

Lisa You're scared of me.

Jack No, just I –

Lisa You are. You're scared of me.

Jack Of course if you can just –

Lisa I'm solid – I'm real – you see – you see – touch me – touch me – what do you feel?

Jack Yeah, solid, real, yeah.

Lisa So I'm here. Nothing happened. You're very tired. You're very stressed. Nobody's running away. Nobody's fading. I'm here with you. We're gonna have the baby together. We're gonna be together – for ever. Yeah?

Jack Yeah. Yeah. Yeah.

Lisa Daddy.

Jack Mummy.

Lisa You feeling alright now?

Jack Yeah.

Whooshing sounds. Flashing lights. She's vanished.

Oh no oh no oh no oh – hello hello hello – oh no, please! Are you there? Are you – oh oh oh oh. Oh please don't do this, oh please, oh – I don't want to be on my own. I don't like being on my own. Oh oh oh.

Flashing and whooshing. Blackout. Full light. **Lisa** *is back.*

Lisa   Can I do the curry now?

Jack   You did it again. You vanished. Faded away and then –

Lisa   You're mad.

Jack   Stop doing it.

Lisa   This is completely mad.

Jack   I want you to stop doing that. I don't like it.

Lisa   I'm not doing anything. I'm living with a freak.

Jack   There's a place up there or down there or in there or . . . somewhere, and you are going there.

Lisa   I have enough of this. I've wanted this baby ever since I was thirteen and now you, you – I'm going out.

Jack   Where?

Lisa   I don't know. Shops. Cinema. Mates. Anywhere.

Jack   But what if you vanish – ? In front of your mates?

Lisa   Not gonna happen. Goodnight.

Jack   Stay here.

Lisa   Why?

Jack   It'll be safer.

Lisa   You're making me frightened.

Jack   With the current circumstances.

Lisa   There are no –

Jack   I'll look after you. Stay. Stay. Stay in the house. How we gonna look after baby if you don't stay in the house?

Lisa   How can we if you keep – ?

Jack   It's not me, it's you who's vanishing.

Lisa   See. See. We're incompatible.

Jack   No no, I do love you, Lees, I do, I just – something's going on – I don't understand but there is something, but I – oh – but I do want the baby so . . .

Lisa   Alright, but – listen – you gotta cut out the funny stuff. I want normal. That's important.

Jack   I'll try to cut out the –

Lisa   Normal. Yeah – I just can't handle. There's a world out there of people and they're all odd. They seem odd. They have like freakouts on buses and stuff. Talk to themselves. Punch strangers. I can't handle that. You're normal. That's why I picked you.

Jack   Course.

Lisa   I gotta have a totally normal baby-father.

Jack   I'm the one. Maybe I'm . . . Tonight means so much I'm just . . . Didn't think I was nervous but maybe I'm . . .

Lisa   Come here.

Jack   Yeah.

Whooshing, flashing etc. **Jack** *rapidly gets out his mobile phone. Starts video recording .* **Lisa** *vanishes.*

Jack   Come on, come on.

Wooshing, flashing etc. **Lisa** *reappears.*

Jack   You did it again.

Lisa   No I never, I was just –

Jack   You did. Look.

He rewinds the images, indicates to **Lisa** *to have a look on the phone.*

Lisa   This is stupid, I'm not gonna just –

Reluctantly, she looks.

Lisa   Oh my God. Thin air and then I . . . that's so frightening. Hold me. Oh babe.

Jack (*holds her*)   I know, I know.

Lisa   Am I solid now? I feel solid.

Jack   You are. You're solid now.

Lisa   What we gonna do? If I'm the kind of person who just vanishes – I don't wanna be the kind of person who just vanishes. I never heard of that . . . people who just . . . Oh.

Jack   Me neither.

Lisa   I want to be here for ever.

Doorbell.

Jack   I'll do it.

He answers it. Enter **Barry** *and* **Stacy***, who is eight months pregnant.*

Barry   Will you tell her, will you tell her – ?

Stacy   Just watch him.

Barry   Will you two tell her – ? Will you tell her – She's got this idea, she's got this really stupid idea –

Stacy   It's not –

Barry   She says that I'm vanishing. She says –

Stacy   He has.

Barry   I haven't.

Stacy   You have. You fade in front of my eyes – you go to nothing.

Barry   Will one of you, both of you, tell her that she is mad? Hormones.

Stacy   I'm not –

Barry People don't just vanish. I try but I – It's the baby playing with her hormones, she doesn't – When women are pregnant they get these . . . Your head gets muddled up. You cry and then you're happy and then I vanish.

Jack Barry, mate –

Barry Yeah? (*To* **Stacy**.) Listen to this –

Jack Barry, mate, it's true. People vanish. Lisa's doing the same. Today I've seen –

Barry Jesus.

Jack Three times. People vanish. I never thought till today. But I've seen it. You can just . . . lose people. They fade to nothing. Empty.

Beat.

Barry (*to* **Stacy**) You set him up to this.

Stacy I didn't do nothing.

Barry Lisa?

Lisa It's true. I'm not a solid person. I'm a person who just . . . goes and comes back again.

Barry You're all mad. What you been doing? Well, I'm not going to vanish. Why am I gonna vanish? I'm not gonna vanish. Not gonna vanish when I got a kid on the way.

Lisa Show him the clip.

Jack Look at this.

He shows **Barry** *and* **Stacy** *the phone clip.*

Lisa See? I go to nothing.

Barry Oh my God . . . Is that what I . . . ?

Stacy Just the same. Same as you.

Barry   Oh no. But I want to be in this world. All the time. I don't want to miss stuff. I'm not choosing to go . . . Do you choose . . . ?

Lisa   I didn't know anything. I thought it was all normal till –

Barry   I wouldn't choose . . . I want to be with you.

Stacy   What if you vanish when the baby's born? Can't have you vanishing once the baby's born. That's not a role model. I want a two-parent family. I gotta have – That's what it's about, isn't it? A mum and a dad. I'm not gonna be a sad cow pushing a kid round by myself. That's not what I –

Barry   Course, course.

Stacy   Feels bad when you're gone.

Jack (*to* **Lisa**)   Yeah – feels really terrible.

Lisa   Stop watching that clip.

Jack   I was just –

Lisa   You are – you're just watching it over and over.

Jack   Well . . .

Lisa   Feels really weird, you doing that.

Jack   Just want to see if maybe there's some . . .

Lisa   Don't. Delete it.

Jack   No.

Lisa   I don't like it. It scares me. Delete it.

Jack   It might – It's evidence.

Lisa   I don't care. It's doing my head in. Give it me. Give it me.

Jack   No.

Lisa   I want it. Don't want you looking at that over and over. Fading disappearing nothing. Fading disappearing nothing. Fading . . .

Barry   She's right.

Jack   Alright, alright. I'll look, look . . .

He goes to delete but whooshing, flashing etc. **Lisa** *and* **Barry** *disappear.*

Jack   Oh. No.

Stacy   Barry! Barry! This is doing my head in.

Jack   How many times it's happened to you?

Stacy   Four, five times since breakfast. This is my sixth.

Jack   Does it get any easier?

Stacy   No. Still hurts. In your gut. Your heart. Whatever. Miss him.

Jack   Yeah – me too.

Stacy   I couldn't ever get used to a vanishing person.

Jack   Maybe we'll have to.

Stacy   I can't.

Jack   But if this is, like, the way it's gonna be . . .

Stacy   Then I just can't handle the way it's gonna be.

Jack   You'll have the kid.

Stacy   If it's a stayer. Maybe the kid'll be a vanisher too.

Jack   S'pose.

Stacy   If the dad's a vanisher then maybe the kid's a vanisher too.

Jack   You still want it?

Stacy   Yeah, only . . .

Jack   You'll cope whatever, won't you? Vanisher or stayer?

Stacy   I suppose I don't – this is so new. Vanishers. Stayers. I didn't know there was a difference when I woke up this morning.

Jack   Terrible innit?

Stacy   Yeah. Terrible.

Jack   This could be rest of our lives.

Stacy   No.

Barry *and* **Lisa** *reappear.*

Stacy   Back again.

Barry   Did we . . . ?

Jack   You faded away – you dematerialised. You went somewhere –

Lisa   Oh God. What do you think we are – aliens?

Jack   I don't know.

Lisa   I don't want to be an alien or a ghost. Hold me.

Jack   You go out with someone, you live with someone . . .

Stacy   You get pregnant with someone . . .

Jack   And then they turn out to be a vanishing person.

Lisa   Hold me.

Jack   I'm frightened.

Lisa   We're not aliens or ghosts. Hold me. I think we'd know if we were aliens or ghosts wouldn't we, Barry?

Barry   I think so.

Lisa   And we'd let you know, so don't – Hold me. Hold me. Hold me. I'm totally frightened. I'm totally freaked. So don't just look at me like that, staring. Come and hold me.

Jack   I'm sorry.

He holds her.

Lisa   Please don't say those terrible things about us.

Jack   Sorry.

Lisa   Give me a kiss.

Jack   . . . I can't. Not yet. Sorry, babe.

Lisa   Oh. I just can't take this. It's doing my head in. I got a kid on the way. But you won't even kiss me. It's too . . .

Whooshing, flashing etc – **Lisa** *vanishes.*

Jack   Oh my God. This is too much. This is gonna drive me mad. I can feel my mind turning. I'm losing it. Losing it. Aghhhhh!

Stacy   Come on. Shhhh. Shhhh. She'll be back.

Jack   I suppose.

Stacy   They always come back. Barry's always come back. Barry's here. Look, Barry's here.

Barry   That's right. I'm here for you mate, yeah? She's bound to come back. Everyone always comes back.

Jack   So far. What's she up to – up there?

Stacy   Don't know.

Jack   She could be up to anything right now.

Stacy   Well, I suppose.

Jack   Aliens. Aliens experiment on you, don't they? Oh yeah. I've seen it in documentaries. They abduct you, abduct you up to their spaceship and experiment on you. They could be putting an alien baby inside her. Taking out my baby and . . .

Stacy   I don't think Barry's been experimented on, have you?

Barry   No. I'd feel it wouldn't I? I feel like myself. I feel normal. It's you lot act different when I come back. I don't think there's experiments.

Jack   You don't know that. They'd wipe you.

Pause.

She's been gone a bit long, hasn't she?

Stacy   Not that long.

Jack   Was Barry ever this long?

Stacy   Well, I'm not sure . . .

Jack   It was just a few seconds before. Only ever a few . . .

Stacy   Yeah.

Jack   What if she doesn't come back?

Stacy   She will.

Jack   We don't know that. She could have vanished for ever.

Long pause.

Look, she's not coming, she's not coming back . . . She . . . Oh my God, she's not coming back. I've lost her. I loved her and now I've lost her.

Stacy   Give it a bit more time.

Jack   I think we should do something.

Barry   Give it time.

Jack   It's alright for you – you're one of them. You're an alien or a ghost or whatever, but me and Stace we're normal –

Barry   I'm normal!

Jack   Oh no – you go to the secret places, the secret place of the vanished, you've seen the secret place, you don't come back from there normal. (*To the sky.*) Give her back, send her back, send Lisa back to us . . . come on!

Barry *vanishes.*

Stacy   Barry! Barry! Oh God.

Jack   I'm sorry, Stace.

Stacy   This is stressing me so much. I'm only two weeks off my due date, I shouldn't be stressing like this. This can't go on for ever. Can't live days like this. What we gonna do?

Jack   I dunno – maybe scientists or doctors, maybe they'll sort it.

Stacy   You reckon?

Jack   Or the government.

Stacy   Yeah, right.

Jack   Or, or, or maybe it's like a – those poltergeists –

Stacy   Stupid.

Jack   There'll be something – it'll be okay. Something'll work out.

Stacy   I hope so. Not back though, are they?

Jack   No.

Stacy   You really having a baby?

Jack   Yeah. Want this. Until I got a kid, I'm a kid.

Stacy   Same for me . . . They've not come back.

Jack   They will.

Stacy   Yeah?

Jack   They will and then we're gonna stop this.

Stacy   How we gonna . . . ?

Jack   Maybe if we just hold on to them. Hold on to them really tight and don't let them go.

Stacy   For ever?

Jack Well . . .

Stacy You can't just hold on to someone for ever.

Jack We could try. Just till the vanishing's over.

Stacy Oh.

Jack What?

Stacy Something. Baby moving.

Jack Can I listen?

Stacy Yeah?

Jack I'd like to. (*He listens.*) Oh yeah.

Stacy Really – oooo. Better not be – oooo –

Jack What?

Stacy Contractions. No, I'm alright. Baz has gotta be here if –

Jack Yeah. I'll look after you if –

Stacy Yeah?

Jack Make sure you're up the hospital and that you know if you start –

Stacy But you're not the dad.

Jack No. I know that.

Stacy It's not the same.

Jack All I'm saying –

Stacy It has to be the dad. It has to be Baz.

Jack But if he's not here –

Stacy He's got to be here. I need him here. I want him here.

Jack Yeah, but all I'm saying, if he's vanished for ever –

Stacy He hasn't.

Jack   They're not –

Stacy   Nobody vanishes for ever. (*Clutches stomach.*) Ooooo.

Jack   'Nother listen?

Stacy   It's not a game.

Jack   Please.

Stacy   No.

Doorbell rings. Exit **Jack***. He re-enters with a group of friends –* **Karen, Holly, Tony, Matt, Marie** *– all talking at the same time.*

Karen   Listen, listen. Something's happening. Something's going on. We've all been vanishing. All of us. We were all round Holly's house and then, like, Matt vanished first, didn't you –

Matt   That's right.

Karen   But then Matt came back again. But then it was Marie, James, me.

Tony   And me.

Karen   One at a time until it was like: who's next? Who's going to go next? Stick together guys, cos we don't know who's going to go next.

Holly   We are seriously frightened.

Enter **Ryan***, running after them.*

Ryan   It's happening all over the world.

Karen   Yeah?

Ryan   Been on the news. Everywhere there's people fading away to nothing. They've got footage from China, America, India – everything. Nobody knows the figures. One in ten. That's what they're saying. One in ten people has already gone but the numbers keep going up – with every minute there's more and more.

Jack   There could be nobody.

Karen   Don't.

Jack   By the end of today there could be nobody left.

Marie   Let's pray.

Matt   What's that gonna do?

Marie   We gotta do something. (*Kneels.*) Oh Father who created this world and made everything in it and is now taking away everything in it, have pity on us poor children. Spare us, spare us, spare us.

She continues to mutter a prayer under.

Stacy   I feel so close.

Jack   Yeah?

Stacy   It might happen. What if it happens? I don't want to have my baby like this.

Jack   Shhhh. Whatever it is – we'll cope.

Stacy   I want Barry. Barry! Barry! BARRY!

Jack   Stace – no – you musn't upset yourself – you'll bring it on – Stace!

Stacy   BARRY!

Marie *vanishes.*

Holly   Marie. When's it gonna end?

Megaphone (*off*)   This is the authorities. Stay in your homes. I repeat: stay in your homes.

Jack   Oh my God.

Megaphone (*off*)   Anyone leaving their home without authorisation will be shot. We are investigating the vanishings but you must stay in your homes.

Enter two **Soldiers.**

Soldier 1   Whose house is this?

Jack   Mine.

Soldier 1   The military has taken control. This country is now under military control.

Jack   Oh my God.

Soldier 1 (*raising gun*)   Keep calm.

Soldier 2   No harm will come to you if you do exactly as the army say. We are requisitioning a number of houses in which to herd the civilian population – and your house has been selected as a suitable centre for civilians. Do you understand?

Jack   I think so.

Soldier 1 (*who has been listening on an earpiece*)   They're ready to bring in the other civilians.

Soldier 2   Good – let's get them in here.

Soldier 1 (*calls off*)   In here.

Soldier 2   Your home is to be the base for the parents and babies group. This way, this way.

Soldier 3 *marches in a huge range of different parents and babies: single parents and couples, papooses front and back, and buggies, prams – some with twins, triplets. The noise of crying babies fills the air.*

Soldier 3   That's it – make room, make room – if you squeeze in – you gotta make room.

Soldier 1 (*pointing gun*)   Calm and orderly – that's it.

Soldier 2   Room for everyone.

Finally everyone is in – but it's a very tight squeeze.

Soldier 1 (*with megaphone*)   Everyone sit down. We have to keep order. We have to keep control. Each parent must take responsibility for controlling their baby. No baby is to crawl or in any way move from their buggy or papoose. It is vital that we keep calm. Let's organise entertainment. Can anyone juggle, dance or offer any skills that might amuse the babies?

A **Man** *or* **Woman** *comes forward.*

Wo/man   Me.

Soldier 1   Please entertain the children.

The **Wo/man** *begins to break dance or juggle or play the ukelele – or anything else that might entertain a large crowd of parents and babies. But after a while whooshing, flashing etc.* **Lisa** *appears. The crowd gasps. Entertainment stops.*

Jack   Lees?

Lisa   I got to speak to Jack. Where's Jack?

Jack   I'm here. Are you alright, Lees?

Lisa   No. I'm hurting. Oh!

She collapses.

Jack   Come on, love. It's alright.

Lisa   Who are all these people?

Jack   You did another vanishing, Lees.

Lisa   Yeah?

Jack   Lots of people are vanishing. It's happening all over.

Lisa   Ugh. Hurt.

Jack   We were gonna have a quiet night in, weren't we?

Lisa   It's all gone wrong.

Jack   It'll go back to normal – everything always goes back to normal.

Lisa   It won't. It's not gonna, because . . .

Jack   You'll see, everything'll get sorted. We'll be a family.

Lisa   I want to come back to you – I do.

Jack   You're back now, babe.

Lisa   I'm trying to break through but I can't. I can't stay this time. The pull's too strong.

Jack   Stay, Lees. For ever. I need you here.

Lisa   I can't. I have to go. I loved this world. I loved you. That's all I wanted. But I'm lost to this world. I'm lost to home and shopping and baby and work and you. All that's gone now. I have to be in the other world – I have to –

Jack   Lees – no – don't do that – See all the babies here, Lees? See 'em?

Lisa   Yeah. Pulling back to the other world.

Whoosh, flash. **Lisa** *vanishes. Panic in the crowd.*

Marie   Oh my God, that was so horrible – that was, like, the most horrible thing I have seen in my life ever.

Ryan   Do you think she'll come back?

Jack   Maybe gone forever.

Soldier 2   Order, order – we must have order.

Jack   Lisa? Lisa?! Come back, come back.

Soldier 2   Steady there.

Jack   I love you. I want a baby.

Soldier 2   Stop or I shoot – you're spreading panic.

Jack   But I have to have her. She's everything I need –

Soldier 2 (*raising gun*)   I have permission to shoot troublemakers.

Jack   Shoot me then, go on. What's the point? That's my future just vanished. Better shoot me now. They've all got babies. You've all got babies. That's what I want. Give me a baby. Give me a baby. I want Lisa back so we can have our baby and fill up the world again. Don't you look at me like

I'm nutter. Just cos you got your babies. Could be me. Should be me with a baby.

Whoosh, flash. A third of the people in the room vanish. Pandemonium. Babies howling, parents offering toys and bottles, cooing.

Soldier 1   Everybody calm!

Karen   I don't want to go. I don't want to go. Please don't take me.

Ryan   It's the end of the world. The end of everything.

Holly   This is like the most horrible thing that's happened to me ever.

A young **Mother** *steps forward from the crowd and talks directly to* **Jack**.

Mother   My baby. The pram's empty. Look – an empty pram. My baby was three weeks old. But already her eyes followed me around the room. Baby once. Now – empty pram.

Jack   It'll all come right.

Mother   How do you know that?

Jack   I don't . . .

Mother   There's two languages. You got kids or you haven't got kids. And if you haven't got a kid you don't speak the language. It's a love, it's a something, a –

Jack   Yeah – but –

Mother   Sorry. You're just a kid – you don't understand.

Jack   Maybe. But I'll understand – yeah. Very soon I'll understand when Lisa –

Mother   You'll never get your chance. You missed your chance. This is it. This is the world ending. No more people.

Jack   No.

Mother   You say your goodbyes. Now my kid's gone all I want is I go too. Listen to all them babies crying. Soon be gone now.

Whoosh, flash – total darkness.

Here we go. We're fading away. All fading away.

The room empties of people. Silence.

Jack   Hello? Hello? Anyone there? Anyone there at all?

He uses a lighter to create a little bit of light.

Is there anyone left? Or am I the only person left in the world? No, please don't do that. I don't want to be the only person left in the world. That's horrible. See, I won't know what to do if it's just me, cos I need people to talk to and to do things with. I don't exist if there's no one else. I'm nobody without other people. What are they all doing in the other world? Is there another world? Come on – take me there – I don't want to be like this for ever.

He finds a candle and lights it.

Stacy   Jack – is that you? Have they all gone?

Jack   I don't know.

Stacy   Hello? Hello? They've all gone.

Jack   It's just you and me.

Stacy   In the world – do you think it's just you and me in the world?

Jack   Could be . . . I don't know.

Stacy   What are we going to do, Jack?

Jack   I don't know, Stace.

Stacy   Jack –

Jack   Yeah?

Stacy   I'm contracting.

Jack   What do you mean?

Stacy   The baby. My contractions.

Jack   Are you sure?

Stacy   Yeah – oh – oh – yeah – I'm sure.

Jack   How long have we got?

Stacy   Few hours.

Jack   Maybe they'll come back. Maybe all the doctors and nurses and midwives and everything'll be back in time.

Stacy   Maybe.

Jack   Yeah – we just gotta be brave, we just gotta stick it out and –

Stacy   Oh oh oh oh oh. It's the stress – brought it on. Oh.

Jack   What we gonna do?

Stacy   I don't – oh oh oh oh oh. What if they don't come back?

Jack   They will. They've got to.

Stacy   How do you know that?

Jack   I just . . . believe.

Stacy   But it could be you and me and that's it. We could be the human race.

Jack   No no.

Stacy   Oh. Bigger contractions.

Jack   Can't you control it?

Stacy   No – I can't. I wish I could. But I can't.

Jack (*to sky*)   Please – come back. All of you – come back.

Stacy   Jack – face it. They're not coming back. They're never coming back.

Jack   You're scaring me.

Stacy   This is the world. You and me. And I'm just about to have – Oh – Once my waters break that's it, you're gonna have to – You're doctor and midwife and –

Jack   Why me?

Stacy   Because there's no one else.

Jack   Right.

Stacy   So get ready.

Jack   Yes. Okay, okay. I can do this. I can.

He cuddles **Stacy**.

Jack   You . . . breathe and calm and when you're breathing and calm and –

Stacy   There'll be mess and pain and everything.

Jack   It's okay. I know.

Stacy   You'll have so much to do.

Jack   Both of us.

Stacy   Hot water and towels – kitchen paper and and and –

Jack   When we get to that bit. Breathe.

Stacy   Yeah.

Jack   Stace. Do you think this was how it was meant to be?

Stacy   No, I don't. Do you?

Jack   I don't . . . maybe.

Stacy   No – this is not supposed to be. This is not normal. This is . . .

Jack   The last thing in the world?

Stacy   Yeah.

Jack   We're all alone now. Just you and me. Listen to that. Nothing. Babies, traffic. Nothing. I reckon there's no one. Anywhere. Just you and me.

Stacy   Not for much longer.

Jack   No?

Stacy   New one on the way. Are you ready?

Jack   I don't know.

Stacy   You got to be, Jack. You got no choice.

Jack   Yeah. Okay. I'm ready.

Two

The living room. Six months later. **Jack** *and a baby in a pram.*

Jack (*to baby*)   And once upon a time there was a brand new world. And the world had no people. Until – pop – there were two people. And they were called Jack and Stacy. And after a year there were three people in the world cos along came a baby. And they called that baby Kelly. You're lovely aren't you, Kelly? Yes you are. Your mum's out there somewhere and your mum'll be back soon. And we'll be back together. Family.

Enter **Stacy**, *with a rucksack on.*

Jack   How do you get on?

Stacy   Yeah. Not bad. How's baby?

Jack   Baby's good. Took her feed. Nice sleep.

Stacy *opens the rucksack for his inspection of contents.*

Jack   More beans?

Stacy   Yeah. Sorry. But – look.

She holds up a packet of nappies.

Jack   Brilliant. At last.

Stacy   Yeah.

She takes out a tin of rice pudding and a tin opener and opens it.

Jack   You gonna eat that cold?

Stacy   I been hunting all day.

Jack   You get attacked by them escaped lions again?

Stacy   No, it's the dogs, though. They gone feral. Started hunting in packs. There's a load of them live up the multi-storey car park. You have to watch yourself.

Jack   Still no sign of any humans?

Stacy   No.

Jack   I told you.

Stacy   Got to keep looking.

Jack   Six months – if there was anyone else we'd have found them by now.

Stacy   I suppose.

Jack   Come on, Stace, there can't be –

Stacy   Don't you want people? Don't you want the world?

Jack   I don't know.

Stacy   This can't be just – Why would it just be us?

Jack   Luck. Fate. I don't know.

Stacy   A thousand – a thousand thousand – miles – there's someone else.

Jack   Just you and me and . . . baby. Stace – don't you think we should give her a name?

Stacy   No.

Jack   I mean, six months – 'baby' – it might stunt her development, something.

Stacy　I know, only . . .

Jack　How long you gonna wait?

Stacy　I want to choose it with Baz.

Jack　He's not coming back.

Stacy　Don't say that. They're all coming back.

Jack　Yeah . . . You got blood.

Stacy　It's nothing.

Jack　Show me.

Stacy *shows her hand.*

Stacy　There was a cat and a load of kittens sat on the nappies. We had a fight.

Jack　See. Told you. Animals are still breeding.

Stacy　S'pose.

Jack　She must have met a tom. We gotta look after that.

Stacy　It's nothing.

Jack　I'll bandage it.

Jack *exits,* **Stacy** *eats rice pudding,* **Jack** *re-enters with bandage and TCP etc.*

Jack　Here we go.

He dresses the wound, bandages it while:

They were noisy – humans – weren't they?

Stacy　Those elephants down the road make noise.

Jack　Just a few of them. They're lonely. But billions of human beings. That was terrible. It's good that they went.

Stacy　Don't you miss Lisa?

Jack　Sometimes.

Stacy　I thought you were having a kid.

Jack   Yeah, well, she's gone now.

Stacy   For the moment.

Jack   Six months.

Stacy   But if you're having a kid −

Jack   After six months, you move on.

Stacy   Move on? There's nobody to . . . The world's empty.

Jack   Stace − I get lonely in my bed.

Stacy   Can't help that.

Jack   Sleep with me, Stace.

Stacy   No.

Jack   We don't have to do nothing − just share the bed.

Stacy   It'll lead to stuff.

Jack   It won't. Last two humans − at least we could share the bed.

Stacy   Forget it. It's not gonna happen. Ugh! She needs her nappy changing.

Jack   I'll do it. (*To baby.*) Come on, Kelly, we're going to −

Stacy   What did you call her?

Jack   Nothing.

Stacy   You called her something. Kelly.

Jack   Just till she gets a real name. It's not good for her.

Stacy   Oh no, oh no − that is not Kelly, right? That is baby. And I'm not having you doing anything different? Understand? Understand? Give me baby.

Jack   I'm gonna −

Stacy   Give me − now.

Stacy *exits with baby.* **Jack** *opens a box of cornflakes from the rucksack, starts eating with his hands. Whoosh, flash.* **Barry** *appears.*

Barry   Stace? Stace?

Jack   Baz? No.

Barry   Stace.

Jack   Baz, she's –

Barry   Stace.

Whoosh, flash. **Barry** *disappears.* **Stacy** *re-enters with baby.*

Stacy   Where's them fresh nappies?

Jack   Stace – let's go somewhere. Now.

Stacy   What do you mean?

Jack   The whole world's empty. We could live anywhere. Buckingham Palace. Yeah – let's move. Find somewhere else.

Stacy   We're fine here. She's used to it.

Jack   No – we got to move now. I'll get some things.

Stacy   Don't be mad.

Jack   Make a head start before it gets dark.

Stacy   I'm not going anywhere.

Jack   But it's dangerous here. It's not safe here. Please, Stace.

Stacy   You go.

Jack   Please, Stace, you don't understand –

Stacy   Go.

Jack   By myself?

Stacy   I'm not stupid, Jack. I know what you're up to.

Jack   Don't know what you mean.

Stacy   Playing families.

Jack   No.

Stacy   Well, you're not Dad, see?

Jack   I know, but –

Stacy   So keep away from her. She's my baby. Me. Baz.

Jack   Alright – you look after her by yourself from now on.
I'll hunt for my own food.

Stacy   You do that.

Jack   I will.

Stacy   My baby. You keep off her, Jack. Piss off – piss off,
you – piss off and leave me and my baby in peace.

Jack *reaches into the rucksack and pulls out a bread knife.*

Jack   Right – I gave you a warning. This is what we're
doing. I'm taking charge. We're moving on. Pack a few things
and get down here in ten minutes and we move on or I cut
you –

Stacy   Go on, then. Cut me. I don't care.

Jack   I will.

He grabs her by the wrists.

Where do you want cutting first?

Stacy   Jack, don't.

Jack   This is a perfect world. Not having that ruined. You're
not spoiling it for me, Stace. You get born – you think the
world's your mum, your dad, your brothers, sisters. That's
nice. Then you go to school. You got your mates. And that's
good. The world's getting better and getting bigger. Then
you go on holiday – see all these other places. Bigger and
bigger. Then you get on the net and you start chatting and
you got friends all over the world. You ever used to do that in
the old days, Stace – before the vanishing? Chat to people all
over the world?

Stacy   Course. Get off.

Jack   And I thought that was great. Chatting all over the world. But then they go – they vanish, they start to fade away and there's just you and me, and me and Kelly.

Stacy   She's not called –

Jack   She's called Kelly – (*Waves knife.*) Alright?

Stacy   No, I don't wanna –

Jack *slices across her cheek.*

Stacy   Oooooo!

Jack   Kelly. I name our child Kelly. Kelly – tonight, from this moment on, now and for ever more you are christened Kelly. No godparents. But – what can you . . . ? Kelly. Kelly. (*To* **Stacy**, *wielding knife.*) Yes? Yes? Yes?

Stacy   Yes. Kelly.

Jack   That's it, Mummy. Say 'Hello, Kelly.'

Stacy   . . . Hello, Kelly.

Jack   Tonight, Kelly – Mummy and Daddy are going to have a lovely meal of all the food that Mummy got up the shops then when Mummy and Daddy are feeling nice and tired they are going to go to a big house somewhere a long way away, somewhere like Buckingham Palace, with a big double bed –

Stacy   No.

Jack   – big double bed, and they're going to take their clothes off and they're going to get into the big double bed. And they'll hold each other all night. Mummy's been too shy since you were born to sleep with Daddy but tonight she's not going to be shy. Tonight she'll get over that and she'll hold Daddy. And maybe if the mood's right they'll have sex. Yeah – maybe if it's an extra special night they'll have sex. Yeah. They'll have sex.

Stacy   I'm not gonna do that.

Jack   You'll do just what Daddy tells you to do or I'll –
Because this is all for Kelly, this is all. We got to be normal.
Normal family. In a normal family – baby's got a name,
Mummy and Daddy love each other, Mummy and Daddy
have sex, Mummy and Daddy try for another baby.

Stacy   No.

Jack   Kelly all on her own. Not good. Not right. So we start
working on a little brother or little sister for Kelly. We start
working on that tonight.

Stacy   It's not gonna happen.

Jack   It's the normal thing.

Stacy   Then I'm not going to be normal.

Jack   You are.

He slices at her cheek.

Stacy   Don't, Jack – no. Is there blood?

Jack   A bit.

Stacy   I'll go septic and die.

Jack   No.

Stacy   Yeah. I'll go septic and die, and then what you
gonna do?

Jack   I'm here for you. I'm here for us all. I'm gonna mend
this and then you're gonna pack our stuff and we're gonna
move on to our new place. Go and pack.

Stacy   I'm gonna change baby. Kelly. Don't hurt her. You
can hurt me, only . . .

Jack   I'd never do that. She's everything to me.

Stacy   Alright, as long as . . .

Jack   I know what's best. I'm Dad.

Stacy   Yeah.

She exits with Kelly. Whoosh, flash. **Barry** *appears.*

Barry   Where's Stace . . . ?

Jack   Still . . . a long way away . . . hunting.

Barry   My kid. Want to see my kid.

Jack   Listen, Baz. I gotta tell you . . .

Barry   Yeah?

Jack   World's gone bad . Streets are full of wild animals. Baz, it's really bad here, you don't wanna – The world's such a bad place, Baz . . .

Barry   Yeah?

Jack   And . . . It's been six months. World moves on.

Barry   Well . . . yeah.

Jack   There's no one left in the world, Baz – 'cept me and Stace and Kelly. Oh yeah. We called the kid Kelly.

Barry   But I wanted to –

Jack   Sorry, mate. I delivered the baby. Pain like you wouldn't believe for hours. Stace screaming in your face. I found the baby – guided it down. First pair of hands to guide it. Cut the cord. Cleaned them up – mother and kid. I chose the name. I like it. See, and now . . . we got a bond. Stacy. She's mine.

Barry   No.

Jack   And Kelly – we decided it was best, too confusing see. Not gonna tell her about the world before, the vanished people. Decided to tell Kelly I'm her dad. Mummy, Daddy and baby.

Barry   You bastard.

Jack   Maybe. But that's the way things are. So the rest of you can stay up there or down there or out there or whatever

because we don't want you. You're not wanted here. So you
stay right where you –

Barry   No!

He punches **Jack** *in the stomach.* **Jack** *collapses.* **Barry** *kicks him.*

Barry   My kid. My world.

Jack   Don't want you. Stay in your world, cos this world's
better without you. I'm king here.

Whooshing, flashing. **Barry** *vanishes.* **Jack** *is winded. Gets up.*

Jack   Alright, alright, everything's okay. Over now.

Enter **Stacy** *with a shopping trolley fully loaded with bags etc, wearing
a coat.*

Stacy   Did what you said.

Jack   Good girl.

Stacy   Think it's best, innit? If I do what you say?

Jack   I don't like forcing you.

Stacy   Funny way of . . .

Jack   Only sometimes I just see. What's best. For the family.

Stacy   Right.

Jack   You'll like Buckingham Palace.

Stacy   I'll do what you say.

Jack   Stace – you gotta love me.

Stacy   That an order?

Jack   That should come natural.

Stacy   Well – it's not natural.

Jack   Give it time.

Stacy   No. Anything you want you'll have to use that (*knife*).

Jack   If I have to.

Stacy   Yeah, you have to.

Jack   Princess Kelly's gonna have her own apartments when she's older. Her own wing. Kensington Palace.

Stacy   Let her choose.

Jack   She'll need guiding.

Stacy   Oh. Like we all do – yeah?

Jack   Wagons roll.

He puts the baby in the pram starts to push it.

Come on, Kelly. New home. New start.

Stacy   Oh, I – (*She staggers.*)

Jack   What?

Stacy   I – I – I – (*She collapses.*)

Jack   Gotta move. Gotta move on. Come on. Gotta get up. Come on.

Stacy   Jack – I'm – oh!

Flashing. Brief vision of the hordes of the vanished. Whooshing. Dies down. **Stacy** *has vanished. Just* **Jack** *and the baby left.*

Jack   Right. Right.

Pause.

(*To baby.*) Just you and me. Which is . . . this is . . .

Pause.

Once there was a new world. And there was just me in it. And I was all alone. And I grew up. And then one day this baby – pop. I called her Kelly. I looked after her. I fought off the animals. I hunted. I had meaning. I was a king and there was a princess.

That's good, isn't it? We're the first and one day there'll be – pop pop – from nowhere, more babies but until then . . .

Yeah. You and me. Empty world.

Right. We'll . . . sleep here tonight. We'll move on in the morning.

Night, Kelly.

He leans into pram, kisses baby.

Night.

And we all slept sound cos we were the only two in the world and there was no fighting.

He lies down to sleep, closes his eyes. Flashing, whooshing. He leaps up.

Kelly!

Brief vision of **Stacy** *and* **Barry** *carrying away the baby. Whooshing, flashing dies down.* **Jack** *is alone.*

Jack   . . . Empty pram. Empty world.

Long pause.

I was born into this place of the animals and of the shops and the food and the houses.

And I was the only person. The first and the last.

And so I never thought about it. How could I ever think – ? If you never knew there were others, then . . .

But sometimes I dreamt, I imagined there were others. Somewhere – others.

Something in this (*pram*).

But that was fantasy. Because the world is just me. Now and for ever. And on and on and good good good.

Only ever me.

So why the – (*pram*)?

A thing from long ago.

He beats the pram rhythmically.

Don't need you. Never need you. Don't know what you're for. You're for nothing.

Nothing. Nothing. Nothing.

You are . . . a dead thing.

He kicks over the pram, carries on kicking it.

You are a totally dead thing.

I am everything.

I am the world.

So I . . .

Hunt. Eat. Sleep. Move on. This is my world.

And I . . .

No, if there were never others then there's no loneliness.

No lone . . . lone . . . lo . . . lo . . .

Lugh. Lugh. Lugh. Lee. Negh. Sssssss.

(*Ape like.*) Ugh ugh ugh.

He's becoming more animal, his centre of gravity moving down.

I ugh oh a oh a ooo m a ugh.

Me.

Me.

Me.

Pattern of movement, almost dancing.

Me.

Me.

Me.

And I.

And I.

And I.

He is on all fours, snuffling and whining. A great animal howl. Then the energy drains from him. Finally, he curls up.

Flashing, whooshing. **Soldier 1** *appears, brandishing gun.*

Soldier 1   Hello? Hello?

Jack *wakes, snarls.*

Soldier 1   What the – ? What is this place?

Jack *growls, squats, ready to attack.*

Soldier 1   Steady. Steady! – I'll shoot.

Jack *bares his teeth.*

Soldier 1   Animal.

He goes to fire.

You had your warning.

Jack *leaps at* **Soldier 1**, *biting at him and snarling. A tussle on the ground. Whooshing, flashing. The room begins to fill up with the vanished.* **Jack** *retreats. Soon the room is full of the parents and babies, the soldiers, the friends and* **Barry**, **Stacy** *and* **Lisa**. *Everyone is talking, calling out. The* **Mother** *with the empty pram steps forward.*

Mother   My kid. My kid. Where's my kid?

She disappears into the crowd, searching.

Holly   Has it finished? Is it over? Have all those people stopped vanishing?

Soldier 2 *comes forward, listening on his earpiece.*

Soldier 2 (*on megaphone*)   Attention. I have received instructions that it is over. The emergency is now over. The vanished have returned. You are to go back to your homes. There will be a period of transition in which the army will be guiding you. But democracy will return. Back to your homes. Go back home. Normality will be restored. The world is normal again.

Jack *is whimpering on the floor.*

Soldier 2   What happened to this one?

Soldier 1   Feral. Mad. I can shoot him.

Soldier 2   No – leave him there. Alright, come along, everybody – back to your homes.

The room is clearing. **Lisa** *comes forward from the crowd.*

Lisa   Jack, it's me – Lisa. Do you know me – Lisa?

Jack   Mmmmgrrrmmrrr.

Lisa   Lisa.

Jack   I. Me. Duh. Duh. Mad. Mad.

Lisa   You're not mad, Jack. Look at all the people. Babies.

Jack   Uh grrrroooo ooo.

Lisa   No, I wanna human.

Stacy *comes forward. She is eight months pregnant.*

Stacy   You alright, Jack?

Jack   Grrrrrrr. Grrrrrrrr.

Stacy   Jack – what's happened to you?

Jack   Grrrrrrrrrrrrrrr.

Stacy   You're frightening.

Barry   Come on love. Keep away.

Stacy   Oooo. Felt something. I reckon this baby might come early.

Barry   Shall we pick names?

Stacy   Tonight? (*To* **Lisa**.) Good luck.

Barry *puts his arm around* **Stacy** *and they exit. It's just* **Jack**, **Lisa** *and the* **Mother** *with the empty pram.*

Lisa   Come on Jack. Human words.

Mother   I got no baby. Pram's empty.

Lisa   What you gonna do?

Mother   Search. It hasn't vanished.

Lisa   Could have.

Mother   No. I'm a mother. I've gotta find her.

Jack   L–l–l–listen.

He stands upright, human.

Th–th–th–there's . . . yeah . . . There's a place where people go to. They vanish. The people who . . . yeah.

Mother   I'll go there and bring her back. I'll carry on.

Exit **Mother** *with empty pram. Just* **Jack** *and* **Lisa**.

Lisa   We're all back . . . Are you human?

Jack   Human. Yeah.

Lisa   Good. I'm hungry. Is there food?

Jack   Lees. Where did you go?

Lisa   Nowhere. Emptiness. It's a blank.

Jack   Think. Underworld? Spaceship?

Lisa   I can't . . .

Jack   Parallel . . . ?

Lisa   You can ask as many times as you like.

Jack   You gotta remember something.

Lisa   I don't. When you vanish there's nothing.

Jack   Maybe you'll get flashes or dreams or . . . ?

Lisa   Jack. Empty.

Jack   It'll come back. One day you'll know what there is.

Lisa   Maybe.

Jack You'll tell me. It's important.

Lisa What did you do?

Jack Eh?

Lisa Six months on the planet. What did you do?

Jack I don't know . . .

Lisa You're the only human being who knows.

Jack I – Nothing.

Lisa Yeah?

Jack Did what I could to survive. Went out hunting. Did what I could for Stace and the baby. There was a baby. Until now. She's . . . She's regressed. Hasn't had . . . But there was a baby then. I kept things going. Fought. Protected.

Lisa Like an animal?

Jack You have to.

Lisa They'll be rebuilding the world now.

Jack No more rhinoceros up the shopping centre.

Lisa So you can be a human being, yeah?

Jack Do my best. Do you think it was aliens?

Lisa Stop.

Jack Maybe if you tried drawing or –

Lisa Just stop.

Jack Hypnosis to –

Lisa Stop. Stop. Stop. Listen. You are never going to know. Face it. It's not going to –

Jack The mother of my – everyone's been there. Secret. And I don't know it. It's impossible. Can't live with that.

Lisa There's no choice.

Jack   I want to see inside their heads, their memories –

Lisa   No.

Jack   Cut 'em open: 'Where did you go? Where did you go? Where did you go?'

Lisa   Stop it, Jack – you're horrible.

Jack   How am I supposed to spend the rest of my life with you if you got a secret?

Lisa   It's not a –

Jack   I can't do that.

Lisa   If you want you can go. Leave. There's the door.

Jack   Yeah.

Lisa   You can pack and leave if that's how you feel.

Jack   Maybe.

Lisa   Run off.

Jack   Yeah.

Lisa   Go on.

Jack   Yeah. That's best. If I never know you . . .

Long pause.

Lisa   You're still here.

Jack   I know.

Long pause.

I know.

Long pause.

Yeah.

Long pause. He touches her stomach.

Yeah.

Totally Over You

Note

This play was suggested by a one-act play by Molière. In *Les Précieuses ridicules*, two young women reject their suitors because they do not have courtly manners, manners which Molière believed were affected and stifling of humanity. Like Molière's play, mine is written to be played on a bare stage. The scenes are not set anywhere and need no scenery or furniture – nothing to suggest a location. Which sounds abstract on the page but plays very naturally. And makes sense of Molière's humanism. It's the person that counts not the illusions – be it courtly manners or celebrity – they fool themselves with.

A mark in the dialogue like this / is the cue for the next actor, creating overlapping dialogue.

Characters

Kitty
Rochelle
Hannah
Sinita
Letitia
Donna
Rachel
Indu

Jake
Dan
Tyson
Framji
Victor
Michael
Rubin

Members of a drama class

One

Enter **Kitty** *and* **Jake**.

Kitty Don't laugh, Jake, don't laugh at me.

Jake I'm sorry, Kit. But when you talk about celebrity.
When you tell me that you and Roche and H and Sin are
going to be famous –

Kitty We are.

Jake I have to laugh.

Kitty Because . . . ?

Jake Because . . . in six months – six months when
I thought we'd told each other all our secrets – six months
and you've never told me that –

Kitty And when I do you laugh at me.

Jake I'm sorry, Kit.

Kitty I choose to share my dream with you and you mock.

Jake I shouldn't but . . . I just never knew. Tell me. Tell me
what you dream about.

Kitty You musn't laugh.

Jake I won't.

Kitty Even a giggle and I'll stop.

Jake I promise. I want to understand girls. I want to
understand what goes on inside their heads I want to know
what you talk about. You and Roche and H and Sin. Tell me.
Tell me about your dream.

Kitty Okay. We're going to be celebrities. Pretty soon,
you're going to see us everywhere. Huge billboards with our
faces on a thousand feet high. TV screens with us talking,
moving, dancing, laughing. The front pages will tell you what
we're up to every day. If we choose the swordfish over the
caviar in a restaurant they're going to analyse it live on CNN.

You go to buy a can of Coke – they'll have our faces on the side. Whole coachloads of Japanese schoolkids are going to dress like us. Your screensaver, your desktop, your mobile's welcome screen – all of them will be me and Roche and H and Sin.

Pause. Then **Jake** *laughs.*

Kitty   Oh piss off, Jake. Just piss off.

Jake   I'm sorry, Kit. I just – you know.

Kitty   What?

Jake   Look at us. This town, this school. It just seems such a fantasy.

Kitty   An ambition. That's the trouble with you, Jake. You don't want anything.

Jake   I want –

Kitty   I am so fed up with you.

Jake   I'm sorry, I'll –

Kitty   I don't want to see you any more.

Jake   What, you're – ?

Kitty   I'm ending this relationship. Here. Now. Goodbye.

Jake   No. Kit. Wait. You can't just walk away.

Kitty   Why not?

Jake   Because I love you.

Kitty   That's nice.

Jake   And you love me.

Kitty   Do I? Do I really, Jay? I don't think so. No. I think I used to. But I'm growing up fast. Six months ago I was a kid and now . . .

Jake   Now you're a celebrity.

Kitty   Now I'm ready to be a celebrity. And I don't need you any more. So – there. I'm freeing you.

Jake   Kitty, please.

Kitty   You're a nice guy. You're good-looking. Ish. You have a sense of humour. Someone else will go out with you.

Jake   No.

Kitty   Goodbye. I'm not your girlfriend any more.

Jake   I've still got the photo of you up beside my bed. The photo I put up the day I asked you out and you said yes.

Kitty   You have to go now. Rochelle's on her way over and we've got a lot to talk about.

Jake   Plans for the future?

Kitty   Sort of.

Jake   So what now? Talk to your stylists? Talk to your PR people? Sort out a few shoots? A few interviews?

Kitty   Piss off, Jake.

Jake   Or maybe you're just going to sit here with *Heat /* and *Hello* –

Kitty   No, actually, no.

Jake   Sit here and waste your time with pointless, pointless dreams?

Enter **Rochelle**.

Rochelle   Hi, guys.

Jake   What are you going to be?

Kitty   How do you mean?

Jake   In five years, ten years, twenty years. What are you two going to be?

Kitty   I told you, Jacob. Celebrities.

Rochelle   That's right.

Jake   Are you going to be in a band?

Kitty   Maybe. I don't know.

Jake   Or act?

Kitty   Yeah. Could do.

Jake   Or model or present on MTV or – ?

Kitty   Yeah, yeah. Jake –

Jake   Well – which one? What's going to make you famous?

Kitty   I don't know. I don't care. / It doesn't matter.

Jake   You've got to have a talent. You've got to have a gift.
An achievement.

Kitty   Of course, yeah.

Jake   And I hate to break this to you, girls, but you can't
sing, you can't act, you're okay-looking but you're not
models –

Kitty   We'll find a way.

Jake   Dreaming, the pair of you.

Kitty   You reckon?

Jake   Yeah. Silly, silly girls.

Kitty   Okay. You want to know? You want to know what's
gonna make us famous?

Jake   Yes. I want to know what's going to make you
famous.

Kitty   Okay. We're going to date celebrities.

Rochelle   That's right.

Jake   Oh really?

Kitty   Not boys, not children, not the kids we have to hang around with here, but proper, A-list, friends-of-Elton-John-and-his-partner-David-Furnish celebrities.

Rochelle   That's right.

Jake   Ridiculous.

Kitty   To you. To you. You boy. You infant. But to us. Have you any idea how frustrating it's been, going out with you when you know you should be going out with a star?

Jake   Fantastic. Sleep your way to the top.

Kitty   No, Jake. Love my way to the top. And the top is going to love me. Now can you please go? Roche needs to talk to me, don't you, Roche?

Rochelle   That's right.

Kitty   Roche is majorly upset, aren't you, Roche?

Rochelle   That's right.

Jake   And where are you going to meet him? Where are you going to meet your celebrity?

Kitty   I don't know.

Jake   Just gonna bump into him at the 7–11?

Kitty   Maybe.

Jake   He spills his Fanta over you and the next week you're snogging on a secluded beach on page four of *Heat*?

Kitty   Possibly, yes, possibly.

Jake   You're pathetic, Kit.

Kitty   I hate you, Jake. Freak off. Go on. I don't want you here. It's gonna happen. Today. By the end of a day I'm gonna be dating a celeb.

Rochelle   That's right.

Jake   By the end of today? That's a promise?

Kitty   That's a promise.

Jake   Ha. Ha. Ha.

Exit **Jake**.

Kitty   Loser. We're gonna show him.

Rochelle   Maybe he's right, Kit. Maybe we're never going to make it.

Kitty   No. You know what that horoscope said.

Rochelle   I know.

Kitty   'Cast off old attachments and prepare to live your dreams.' And that's exactly what we've got to do. Did you stick to the plan?

Rochelle   Yeah. I did it just like you said. Only . . .

Kitty   I need you with me, Rochelle. We've got to stick together. Everybody else in this stupid school, this stupid town, is gonna laugh at us, but you and me and H and Sin, we've got to keep on going for each other. Okay?

Rochelle   Okay. Just . . .

Kitty   Yeah?

Rochelle   Dan cried. When I said, 'I don't want to be your girlfriend any more,' he burst into tears. Like great big sobbing tears. And I wanted to say, 'Dan, Dan. Stop. I didn't mean it. I still love you.'

Kitty   But you didn't.

Rochelle   No, Kit. I didn't. Select All. Delete. Just like you said.

Kitty   You had to do it, Roche. Dan's a nice guy . . .

Rochelle   He's a really nice guy.

Kitty   But can you imagine him with David Beckham or Sting or the Queen?

Rochelle No. No, I can't.

Kitty He'd say all the wrong things. And what about his skin?

Rochelle It is a bit zitty.

Kitty Exactly. 'Rochelle and her acne-covered boyf welcome you into their new luxury home.'

Rochelle Yuck. No way.

Kitty We're gonna find you a nice Calvin Klein model.

Rochelle Oh yeah. Skinny but toned.

Kitty And a tattoo like a barcode on his bum.

Enter **Hannah**.

Hannah Oh God. I feel like such a bitch. 'Tyson, this is the end.' He just kept on repeating in this really pathetic voice: 'Why? Why? Why?' Over and over again. 'Why? Why? Why?' And now he wants back everything he ever gave me: CDs, videos, T-shirts. Everything. And I'm going to miss them so much. This better be worth it, Kit.

Kitty Worth it? H. What's Tyson when you are gonna have your pick of film stars, singers, footballers, models? You want Brad Pitt?

Hannah I'd love Brad Pitt but –

Kitty Then work it, girl. We are gonna be so famous he won't resist.

Hannah But isn't he with – ?

Kitty You'll be all over the papers for days. Your publicist will have to work overtime. 'I regret all the hurt I've caused,' you'll say. 'But Brad and I are so happy together.'

Hannah Yes. An intimate wedding. Brad. Our families. And a few friends.

Kitty   That's it. And where's Tyson gonna be? Stacking shelves? The call centre?

Rochelle   Car-park attendant maybe.

Kitty   Let him read about it in the papers.

Hannah   Brad and I are gonna meditate for an hour together every morning.

Rochelle   And have tantric sex together for four hours every night.

Hannah   Tantric sex? What's that?

Enter **Sinita**, *crying.*

Sinita   I hate you, Kitty. Why did you make me do that? I love Framji, I do. And now. And now. I finished with him. (*Cries.*)

Rochelle   Come on, babe.

Sinita   He says he never wants to see me again. Or walk down the same street as me. Or take the same bus as me. Or use the same search engine as me. Totally – gone. For ever. And what am I gonna do without him?

Kitty   Do without him? Do without him? You know what you're gonna do without him. Same as me without Jay, same as Roche without Dan, same as H without Ty. Be a celebrity.

Sinita   And are you sure about that, Kit?

Kitty   Yes of course. Totally sure. Aren't you?

Sinita   Well . . .

Kitty   Sin. You can't give up this easily. I know this is hard. But think of the reward. Think of waking up in this totally fantastic house next to your totally buff boyfriend.

Rochelle   And there's a TV crew already there as you open your eyes. They're making a documentary about you 24/7. There's a whole cable channel that shows it all totally live.

Hannah   And then you exercise with your buff personal trainer.

Kitty   Take some conference calls with Japan as you eat your breakfast – they're planning this Barbie-type doll of you to launch in markets right around the world.

Rochelle   The morning: photo-shoots – a calendar. Some fittings for your bridal gown. *Hello* is sponsoring your wedding. Only fourteen months to go.

Hannah   Lunch with Donatella, Beoncye and Madonna. Chatter, chatter. You debate: is hatha yoga now passé? Then cameras: flash, flash, flash.

Kitty   The afternoon: a massage and a meeting with the team from LA who want to turn you into an animated series for TV. You tell them: nice idea, but you're holding out to see what happens with the movie rights.

Rochelle   Then off to a gallery. You've done a painting for charity. Just a fun thing. 'I'm no artist,' you tell the waiting press. 'But I do care about sick children and I just wanted to do whatever I could to help.'

Hannah   And then up the red carpet at a film launch. 'Is it true they're making you into a musical?' 'No comment.' Then party, party. 'Hi, Nicole! Hi, Ewan! Hello, Uma!' Then driven home.

Kitty   And as you fall into your bed you say: 'I did it. This is me. My dream, my hope, my destiny. Celebrity.' Today was hard. I know that, girls. 'Cast off old attachments,' that's hard. But now it's time, time to live your dreams. Are you gonna do that, Sin?

Sinita   Will I have a stalker?

Kitty   Maybe.

Sinita   I'd like a stalker. Someone who fills their house with pictures of me. Goes through my bins. Names all their children after me. Who can't get me out of their head.

Kitty   Of course you'll have a stalker.

Sinita   And threatens to shoot himself if I don't return his calls.

Kitty   Yes. Absolutely.

Sinita   Oh wow.

Kitty   Are we sticking together, girls? Are we sistas?

Rochelle/Hannah/Sinita   Yeah.

Kitty   Then come on. New *OK* out today. New *Sugar*. See what our horoscopes say today.

She produces magazines from her bag and hands them round.

Kitty   Oh my God. Can you believe that? ' "Ooops I ate it again." Britney piles on the pounds.'

Rochelle   She often does that when she's under stress. It's her flaw.

Sinita   My uncle emailed me this video clip of Britney and Justin doing it.

Rochelle   I think actually in her heart she still misses Justin.

Sinita   But maybe it was just lookalikes or something. It was a bit of a shaky camera and the lighting wasn't so good.

Hannah   I bet it was, though. I bet Britney's done it.

Rochelle   Do you think chocolate's a carb?

Kitty   Okay. Horoscope time. Oh my God. Oh my God. Look at this. 'A stranger will show you the way to future happiness today.' What does that mean? Keep your eyes peeled for a stranger, girls.

Enter **Letitia, Donna, Rachel, Indu, Michael** *and* **Rubin.**

Kitty   Ugh, look.

Hannah   Do I see the most uncool people on the whole planet?

Sinita   The whole universe.

Rochelle   Oh no. The drama class.

Indu   Hey, girls, you missed a great drama class today.

Kitty   We've got no time to talk to you guys. We're waiting for a stranger.

Rachel   We all had these numbers and that was the status you were. Status is like a power, yeah a sort of power, influence, status sort of thing.

Sinita   Right.

Rubin   So – say you're a king. Then you're, like, a ten. Unless you're a low-status, sort of nervous king. Then you're like a three or something.

Hannah   Wow. Sounds amazing.

Letitia   And I got a two. Which is really, really low. Like a really awkward, stupid, clumsy sort of person.

Rochelle   Wow, Tish. That must have been hard.

Letitia   Yeah. That's what I thought at first. But then – when I got into it. Wow. I was like this total two.

Kitty   Tish. You're sad.

Donna   Not as sad as you, bunking off so you can –

Sinita   Drama's for losers, Donna.

Michael   But if you wanna be celebrities –

Hannah   And what do they teach us? Improvisation? Theatre games? *Romeo and Juliet*? No thank you. That's not the stuff we need to know.

Rochelle   Yeah. We wanna know how to make love to the camera.

Sinita   How to make the camera love us.

Kitty   How to use a microphone. When to listen to your stylist and when to listen to your instincts.

Hannah   How to handle the press. What dress to choose for a premiere.

Sinita   How to mime in videos, voice-over for an ad.

Kitty   And who's the best agent if you're gonna be a star. But do they teach us that? No.

Rochelle   This is the twenty-first century. Drama's for losers.

Letitia   But I just think it would be so great.

Sinita   What would?

Letitia   To lose yourself. Become another person.

Kitty   That's not the way it works any more, Tish. You're a brand. You sell yourself. You don't become another person.

Letitia   But that's what I wanna –

Kitty   Then you keep going to drama classes. You keep wasting your time with silly games. But me and the girls aren't doing that. Are we, girls?

Rochelle/Hannah/Sinita   No.

Kitty   Come on, girls. Let's find a stranger to show us the way to future happiness. Enjoy the acting, Letitia.

Exit **Kitty, Rochelle, Hannah** *and* **Sinita**.

Letitia   Status ten. Status ten. Status ten. Status one. Status one. Status one.

Exit **Letitia**.

Donna   Tish? Tisha? She is so upset.

Exit **Donna, Indu, Rachel, Michael** *and* **Rubin**.

Enter **Jake** *and* **Victor**.

Jake   Victor. Will you stop following me? I want to be alone.

Victor   But we said we'd go to a movie.

Jake   Yeah. Well. I've changed my mind.

Victor   There's a sci-fi thing. Which sounds good. Or an action thing. Which sounds okay. Or a CGI thing. Which sounds cute. Or a comedy. Which sounds hilarious. Which do you fancy?

Jake   None of them.

Victor   I've got some DVDs if you wanna –

Jake   No.

Victor   Or games. My mum left pizza and some oven chips –

Jake   Vic. I want to be by myself. Please.

Victor   But – why?

Jake   Kit finished with me.

Victor   No way.

Jake   Yeah. She chucked me. So –

Victor   I'm sorry.

Jake   And I just want to go into my room and play Korn and be alone.

Victor   But surely a movie would –

Jake   No, Vic. I'm sorry.

Victor   Or a pizza or just hanging out at Burger King –

Jake   Victor. No.

Victor   Okay. But maybe if we just talked –

Jake   This isn't freaking Oprah or Rikki, okay? It's not: 'Jake – my girlfriend just dumped me.' Then talk, talk, talk and out she comes from behind a freaking screen. And she talks and Oprah talks. And the crowd goes 'Ooo,' and then we hug and I cry. And it's the end and Oprah says: 'When you talk the hurt begins to heal.' Okay?

Victor   Okay.

Jake   Why does everybody want to talk? Confess? To kiss and tell? I hate this freaking world we live in.

Victor   I know you do, Jay.

Jake   These freaking superficial boybands and models and movie stars confessing everything just so they can fill up magazines. It's all shit.

Victor   That's right, Jay.

Jake   Well, I'm not talking. Because no one understands what's happening inside me. No one knows and there's no way I can make them know. And I don't want to make them know.

Victor   But I'm your friend.

Jake   I know and . . .

Victor   All the things we've done together. Things I've done for you.

Jake   But Vic – you're a dork. You've never been out with a girl.

Victor   I'd like to.

Jake   And I don't want to talk to someone who doesn't know anything about girls.

Victor   You know Letitia?

Jake   If you haven't been out with a girl you're a child, Vic.

Victor   She did the Nurse in that scene from *Romeo and Juliet.*

Jake   That's the difference between us, Vic.

Victor   I like Letitia. I keep on having dreams about her. I want to ask her out.

Jake   You're a child and I'm a man.

Enter **Dan**.

Dan   I don't believe it. I just don't believe it. Roche finished with me.

Jake   She chucked you?

Dan   Just sat me down and said: 'I don't want to see you any more. We're finished. Over.' She wants to be a celebrity, Jay.

Jake   Oh my God.

Victor   Do you want to see a movie?

Dan   Where do you get Prozac from? Do you have to go to a doctor?

Victor   I think the action movie could be good.

Dan   Or is it an over-the-counter thing? She's going to be famous and she doesn't want to be seen with a boy like me. Would you call me zitty?

Enter **Tyson**.

Tyson   Bitch. Bitch. Bitch.

Jake   What's that, Ty?

Tyson   Hannah. What a freaking bitch. Chucked me. I've never been chucked. Never. Sure – I've chucked a few times. But I've always done it sweetly. I'm a good chucker, but Hannah – freaking horrible.

Jake   Did she say she wanted to be – ?

Tyson   A celebrity. Can you believe that? I told her: no freaking way, baby. And then she got mad at me and chucked me. I'm just so angry.

Victor   Maybe going to a movie would help?

Tyson   What's he doing here? What are you doing here?

Victor   There's a sci-fi movie –

Tyson   Shut up, Victor, shut up.

Victor   I'm just trying to –

Tyson   Victor!

Victor   Okay. Okay.

Enter **Framji**.

Framji   Guys. You'll never guess. Sin finished with me.

Jake   We know.

Framji   She wants to be a celebrity and –

Jake   We know.

Framji   She says I'm holding her back.

Jake   We know. Same for all of us, Fram. Me and Kit. Dan and Roche. H and Ty. You and Sin. We've all been chucked.

Dan   On the same day.

Tyson   At the same time.

Framji   But – they must have planned this.

Jake   That's right.

Framji   I don't believe it. What a bitch.

Tyson   Yeah. Total bitches. All of them.

Enter **Kitty**, **Rochelle**, **Hannah** *and* **Sinita**.

Kitty   Oh hi. We didn't know you were here.

Jake   Yeah. That's right. We're here.

Hannah   We're looking for a stranger. To show the way to future happiness.

Tyson   Right.

Rochelle   Like it says here. You seen a stranger?

Dan   No. Don't think so. No.

Kitty   Come on, girls. They're not gonna help us.

Exit **Kitty**, **Rochelle**, **Hannah** *and* **Sinita**.

Framji   Did you see that? Didn't even look at me.

Jake We need to show them, guys.

Tyson Yeah. We need to punish them –

Dan We need to hurt them –

Framji To teach them a lesson –

Jake To show them how stupid they are.

Dan But how?

Victor Maybe if I   ?

Dan What's the best way to make them suffer?

Victor Can I – ? I've got an idea.

Tyson Victor. You don't know anything about girls. You go off to the library and let us figure this out.

Framji They're coming back. They're coming this way.

Dan Run.

Jake Stay.

Tyson Hide.

Victor Guys. I'm going to show you – Can I show you? Guys?

Jake, **Dan**, **Tyson** *and* **Framji** *hide as* **Kitty**, **Rochelle**, **Hannah** *and* **Sinita** *enter.* **Victor** *conceals his face.*

Victor The future. The future. I see the future.

Rochelle Ugh. Look. A loony.

Sinita A loony homeless person.

Hannah Ugh. Gross. They don't wash. And they really smell.

Sinita And they get aggressive if you don't give them money.

Rochelle Well, I'm not giving him anything.

Kitty   Girls. Listen for a moment. Just listen to what he's saying.

Victor
    The mortal man walks backward
    His face towards what's gone
    The future is a mystery
    But still he travels on.

Sinita   It's like mad person's talk.

Kitty   No. It makes sense if you listen.

Victor
    But I am not as other men
    Who only see what's done
    My brain is burnt with future lives
    I see the world to come.

The future. The future. I see the future.

Kitty   Who are you?

Hannah   Kit, I think we ought / to be going now.

Kitty   No, no. We've got to talk to him. / Find out –

Rochelle   He's really creepy, Kit.

Sinita   Yeah. I think he may be Dangerous.

Kitty   But girls – if he sees the future –

Victor   I know you. I know you. I know you. I know you.

Sinita   Oh my God. He's going completely mental.

Rochelle   I want another Diet Coke. Let's all go and buy another Diet Coke.

Sinita   Yeah, Roche. Good idea.

Kitty   Girls. We've got to ask him. We've got to make him tell us. What happens to us? How do we get to be celebrities?

Hannah   There's no point asking him. He's a spazza.

Kitty   Stick together, girls. We've got to stick together.

Victor   I know you. I know you. I know you. I know you.

Kitty   Me?

Victor   Everybody knows you.

Kitty   In the future?

Victor   You are famous in the future.

Kitty   Oh my God. That's amazing.

Victor   Your picture is everywhere in the future. A hotel in Bangkok, an iMax in New Mexico, a hologram in Times Square – it's you.

Kitty   I knew it. I knew I was right.

Victor   You are a line of clothes, a cola drink, a fitness video, a salad dressing, a dress-me doll, an arcade game, a mouse mat, a bumper sticker, a syndicated column, a talkshow, an infomercial, the most hits in a day on AOL, a remix, beauty tips, a goodwill ambassador, an eight-page pull-out supplement, a diet plan, a chain of restaurants, a literacy campaign, a sex symbol, role-model superstar. You are live action, animation, computer-generated, holographic, CD ROM, exclusive pictures, pay-to-view. All of them are you and you are all of them. Oh yes I know you. In the future I know you. In the future everybody knows you.

Kitty   And Roche and H and Sin as well?

Victor   And Roche and H and Sin as well.

Rochelle   Oh my God.

Hannah   Oh my God.

Sinita   Amazing.

Victor   The bedrooms that you live in now will be musuems – a shrine for all your fans to come and worship. Coaches will pull up outside your school: 'That's the place. That's where she studied.'

Rochelle   That is so cool.

Victor   Everybody who ever knew you will auction every gift you ever gave them. 'This item personally touched by Kitty.' And everything bought – instantly.

Sinita   What will we be famous for?

Victor   Do you know the band Awesome?

Sinita   No.

Victor   Four boys. The finest voices. Best dance routines. Best power ballads. The four most famous faces of the future.

Kitty   And we're . . . ?

Victor   You date them. And they bring you fame.

Hannah   And when do we meet them? Where do we meet them?

Victor   You've already met them.

Kitty   We have?

Victor   They are here in your town, your school right now. Awesome are amongst you. The four most famous faces of the future, the biggest celebrities the globe has ever known are Jake and Dan and Ty and Framji.

Sinita   But we just . . . Oh no . . .

Victor   Yes?

Rochelle   We just chucked them.

Victor   You . . . ? Oh no. Then you must unchuck them fast. You can't meddle with the future. You have to date them or the future's empty: blank videos, blank ads, blank T-shirts, blank covers on the magazines. Without your faces, everything's a void. Quick, quick. Find your friends. Oh God. It's hurting. When time is bent like this it hurts me. Ugh. Ugh. Put the future right. Go out with Jake and Dan and Ty and Fram. Date Awesome! Agh! Agh! Back on the path or I'll die!

Kitty   Oh my God!

Victor   Before it's too late! Aaaggghhh!

Exit **Kitty, Rochelle, Hannah** *and* **Sinita.**

Framji   Woah! Yes! Yes! Yes! Excellent, Victor!

Tyson   Yeah! Fantastic! Excellent! That was / so cool.

Jake   Brilliant! You are such a / good actor.

Victor   Thank you.

Dan   Yeah. You were totally convincing. Amazing.

Jake   And now. Now we can get our own back.

Tyson   Yeah!

Jake   Now we're going to turn the tables. Cos we know what it's like to want someone, need someone, love someone and be pushed aside. We know that feeling, don't we, guys?

Dan   Oh yeah.

Jake   Well, now it's their turn. They are gonna beg us guys. They are gonna cry and plead and do anything they can to get us back. But we are gonna say: no way. Agreed?

Framji/Tyson/Dan   Agreed.

Jake   Come on then. Let the fun begin.

Jake, Framji, Tyson *and* **Dan** *start to exit.*

Victor   Listen, guys. I've got another idea. Make them look really stupid.

Jake   What's that, Vic?

Victor   Let's play with their minds. These girls want to meet celebrities. Then let's arrange for them to meet a few. Let's make them think they've made it. Then destroy them.

Tyson   Yeah.

Victor   You're going to see those girls looking so stupid.
Follow me.

Enter **Letitia**.

Letitia   Hey. What you up to?

Victor   We're sort of . . . we're gonna do some acting.

Letitia   Acting? I love acting.

Victor   I saw you in that scene. The Nurse.

Letitia   Oh yes. The Nurse. I wanted to be Juliet but . . .

Victor   You want to do some acting with us?

Tyson   Vic. This is a boy thing.

Dan   Yeah, Victor. This is us against them.

Letitia   Who against who?

Jake   Sorry, Vic. But we don't want her involved. No girls.

Exit **Jake**, **Dan**, **Tyson** *and* **Framji**.

Letitia   What do they mean, us against them?

Victor   They just – they've sort of gone off girls.

Letitia   And what about you? Are you off girls?

Victor   Oh no. I'm on girls. I mean I like girls. I like a girl.

Letitia   Yeah?

Victor   Listen, if you wanna do the acting with us –

Letitia   Okay.

Victor   I'll try and persuade them. I'd like to give you a big
part. And we'll need the drama class as well. We'll need lots
of people.

Letitia   Are we putting on a play?

Victor   A sort of a play. Well, more a sort of a concert.
A play-concert-media-event sort of . . . you'll see.

Letitia   Okay. Victor –

Victor   Yeah?

Letitia   Nothing.

Exit **Victor** *and* **Letitia.**

Two

Enter **Hannah** *and* **Tyson.**

Hannah   Ty. Just listen for a moment. One moment –
please. I made a mistake. I made the biggest mistake of my
life. But we all make mistakes. And I was mad to finish with
you. I don't know why I did that. Some sort of fever in the
brain. But now – I miss you so much. I want you back so
much. Ty, please –

Tyson   H. I don't got time to talk about this now.

Enter **Letitia,** *in disguise.*

Letitia (*on mobile*)   Yeah. He's here. Yeah he's right here in
front of me. Is he okay? I don't know? (*To* **Tyson.**) Excuse
me, sir. Are you okay?

Tyson   Yeah, sure. I'm okay.

Letitia (*on mobile*)   He's with a girl. Yeah. No. Not so pretty.
Well, I don't know. I don't know if she's bothering him. (*To*
Tyson.) Is she bothering you, sir?

Tyson   No. That's okay.

Letitia (*on mobile*)   Of course I'll pass that on. Five minutes.
Okay. Bye now. Bye. (*To* **Tyson.**) Sorry about that, sir. The
stylist is ready for you, sir. Is that okay with you, sir?

Tyson   That's fine. Are the rest of the guys – ?

Letitia   On their way, sir.

Tyson   I'll be through in just a minute.

Letitia   Certainly, sir. Sorry to interrupt, sir.

Exit **Letitia.**

Hannah   Ty – who was that?

Tyson   My PA. It's kinda embarrassing. But essential. You get used to it.

Hannah   And the stylist?

Tyson   You don't know? H, so much has happened since we split. Me and the guys formed a band. Awesome. Like the name?

Hannah   I love it. It's brilliant.

Tyson   And we've signed to a major label. And the record company have invested a lot of money and today's the day they launch us. Meet the press. Photo-ops. Promote our first single. 'So Totally Over You.' I think you're gonna like it.

Hannah   Yeah. Sounds great.

Tyson   We weren't sure at first whether we wanted the whole celebrity thing, you know? I think that could really play with your mind.

Hannah   Oh definitely, yeah.

Tyson   We talked about it for a long time. How are we going to handle being totally massive? But then we decided to give it a go. Have a laugh. Get rich. Can't be so bad, can it?

Enter **Letitia.**

Letitia   I'm sorry, sir. The stylist?

Tyson   On my way.

Exit **Letitia.**

Tyson   Don't do anything I wouldn't do.

He exits.

Hannah   Tyson. Tyson. Just you freaking come back here.

Enter **Sinita** *and* **Framji**.

Sinita   No, no, no, please. Listen to me. Listen. Just give me a chance. One date. And if that doesn't work out −

Framji   Sin − I've got no time for this. I have a career to launch. Have a good life. Ciao.

Exit **Framji**. *Enter* **Rochelle** *and* **Dan**.

Dan   I'm late. I'm late. I'm late. Call me. No don't. I changed my number. Mail me. No don't, I've changed the address.

Rochelle   Dan, we have to talk.

Dan   Leave a message with Mum. My manager talks to her once a week. She passes on the messages. Most of the time.

Rochelle   Dan −

Dan   The stylist is gonna kill me.

Exit **Dan**. *Enter* **Jake** *and* **Kitty**.

Jake   Kitty. Join the fan club, visit our web page. Have you any idea how busy our schedule is? Buy the single. It rocks.

Exit **Jake**.

Kitty   Bastard. God. They are such bastards. Some people just can't handle celebrity. When we're famous we're really gonna stay in touch with our roots. We are gonna keep it real. Why can't they keep it real?

Hannah   Maybe if you hadn't made us chuck them in the first place . . .

Sinita   Yeah, Kit. I would still have been with Framji if it weren't for you.

Rochelle   And I'd have Dan.

Kitty   But the horoscope −

Rochelle   Shut up about that freaking horoscope, Kit. We've lost them, Kit.

Kitty   No.

Sinita   Yeah. They're great big megastars and we're just schoolkids hanging around.

Kitty   No way.

Enter **Letitia**.

Letitia   I'm sorry. You girls are going to have to move. We have a press launch here in a few minutes.

Kitty   We're with the band.

Letitia   Oh no. If you're with the band I have you on my list here. See? Hair Stylist, Make-Up Stylist, Style Stylist, Personal Shopper, Personal Trainer, Press Aide, Vocal Coach, Dance Coach, Runner. You have to be on the list.

Kitty   What about girlfriend? Is that on the list?

Letitia   Girlfriend? No. Their management won't let them have girlfriends.

Kitty   But they have to have girlfriends. Who's gonna sit beside them on their *Hello* cover?

Hannah   Who's gonna help them out of the Met bar when they've drunk too many vodkas?

Sinita   Who's gonna have their babies? Winter-Storm and Hawaiian Breeze?

Letitia   You're thinking of a more mature market. These guys are for the pre-teens. The pre-teens want them single. Look at the focus groups.

Enter **Michael***, disguised as a stylist, with several assistants carrying clothes.*

Michael   Blinding. These boys look blinding. You wanna see the Polaroids?

He passes some Polaroids to the girls.

Hip and yet High Street, Now and yet For Ever, Sexy and yet Clean, More Than a Boy Not Yet a Man. Great, yeah?

Rochelle   Oh my God, that's Dan. Look.

Sinita   And Framji. Wow. Amazing.

Hannah   Brilliant.

Letitia   They're here. They're here. The press are here. You're going to have to go.

She exits.

Kitty   Can we borrow some clothes from you? We have to blend in or they'll throw us out.

Michael   They're due back with Donatella in an hour.

Kitty   Just half an hour. Please.

Michael   All right. Half an hour and I'm taking them back.

Kitty   Thank you. Thank you. We are gonna look fabulous.

Exit **Michael, Kitty, Rochelle, Hannah, Sinita** *and stylist's assistants.*

Enter **Jake** *and* **Dan**. *They have been 'styled'.*

Dan   So you're saying . . . ?

Jake   I'm saying . . . that Kitty looked really sad.

Dan   Which is kind of the idea, isn't it?

Jake   Which is kind of the idea, yes.

Dan   Your idea.

Jake   My idea. Yes. Just . . .

Dan   Yes?

Jake   I didn't realise . . . she looked so . . . lost.

Dan   Jay. Think how much she hurt you. You can't go back now. Kitty is a bitch, okay?

Jake   Yeah. Kitty is a bitch. Kitty is a bitch. Kitty is a bitch.

Enter **Letitia**.

Letitia   What are you doing here? You should be backstage.

Exit **Jake** *and* **Dan**.

Enter **Donna**, **Rachel**, **Indu**, **Rubin** *and others disguised as the press: reporters, photographers, TV crews.* **Letitia** *organises them.*

Enter **Victor** *in disguise.*

Letitia   Ladies and gentleman, we have a very special new brand for you today. A brand for a multi-market environment. A brand with fantastic synergistic potential. Ladies and gentlemen, brand manager Karl Watkins.

Victor   You know, when I started out in this business it was easy. You found a few boys who could sing. Or looked good. And you gave 'em a few songs. And you bought them a place in the charts. And they went massive. And we all got very rich. Nowadays, of course, it's all a lot more complicated. The market's fragmented. There's video games and web sites and Class A drugs competing for the kids' pocket money. Some mornings I wake up and I say: 'Victor, this is a young man's game. And you're a fat old bastard.' But every now and then, once in a decade, something happens and I get excited about Pop all over again. And my life has meaning. Ladies and gentlemen, does your life have meaning? It does now. Here's Jay, Dan, Ty and Framji. Here's Awesome.

Applause. Enter **Jake**, **Dan**, **Tyson** *and* **Framji**, *with several big security guards (again members of* **Letitia**'s *drama class in disguise) standing by them.*

Jake   Hi. This is our first single. Hope you like it.

Music. They sing: 'So Totally Over You'.

> Used to feel this pain would never end
> Used to think my heart would never mend
> Used to pray that you'd come back to me
> The nights were long

But now I'm free
Cos I grew strong
And baby can't you see?

Chorus:

 I'm so totally over you
(Never want to see your face again)
I'm so totally over you
(Don't need a lover, don't want a friend)
You said goodbye when I was true
Found breaking up was hard to do
But I'm totally over you.

Enter **Michael, Kitty, Rochelle, Hannah, Sinita** *and stylist's assistants. The girls have been dressed in the most impractical high-fashion clothes imaginable.*

We both must go our separate ways
You'll hurt another boy someday
And maybe I will love again
And learn to trust but girl, till then –

Repeat Chorus to fade.

Applause.

Victor   Any questions for the boys?

During the press conference hands are raised and **Victor** *chooses whose questions get answered.*

Donna   Where did the band begin?

Jake   Well, it actually began when my girlfriend chucked me.

Donna   Really?

Jake   Yeah. I'd been going out with this girl. And . . . this is really difficult to talk about. But. I loved her so much, you know? I couldn't stop thinking about her all the time. I couldn't imagine living without her. And then one day she finished with me. Just like that. Over. And I had all this hurt

inside me. And it wouldn't come out. And it kept on hurting
and hurting and it was growing bigger and bigger inside me
like this great big ball of hurt. And then one day I started to
hear this tune. And then I got these lyrics. And I wrote them
down. And I started to feel better. And that's when I wrote
'So Totally Over You'.

Dan   And Jay came to me. Because I'd just had the same
experience. This girl I totally adored had dumped me. And
he said he'd got this song. And he sang it to me. And I really
related to it. Cos that's how I felt. All that hurt. And I heard
like all these harmonies and I wrote them down.

Framji   And then they sang me the song. And it made me
want to dance. Because I'd been chucked too – by this girl
who I thought was the most amazing thing to ever walk the
planet. And I found if I danced it sort of let all the hurt out.
And so I worked out all the choreography.

Tyson   And the guys came over to mine. Because I was
really hurting too after my break-up. And they sang the song,
the harmonies, did the dance, and I was like 'Awesome'. And
that's how we got the name.

Sinita   What would you say to those girls if they were here
today?

Dan   Thank you.

Sinita   Really?

Dan   Yeah. I'd thank them. Because if we hadn't been
chucked like that we wouldn't have had anything to write
about.

Hannah   And what about the lyrics of the song? Would you
say they're true? Could you honestly say to those girls 'So
Totally Over You'?

Tyson   Oh yeah. That's our message to those girls. If she
were here now I'd say: 'Hannah, I'm Totally Over You.' And
I'd say: 'Thing is, H, even if I did still love you – even if, deep
in my heart, I was still in love with you – I couldn't go out

with you. I mean, I'm a celebrity now, right? I have to date other celebrities. And you're not.' I'd say: 'H, you're a wannabe. I can't date a girl like that. You're a nothing to me now.' That's what I'd say if she were here today.

Hannah   Bastard. Freaking freaking bastard.

She exits.

Framji   Yeah, me too. If she was here now I'd be like, 'Stop crying, Sin. Crying's not gonna change anything. Because I don't feel anything. I feel nothing for you. Totally Over You.' That's what I would say to Sinita. If she were here today.

Sinita   Fram, no.

She exits in tears.

Dan   And Rochelle. I'd like to say: 'Had a few good times. Had a few bad times. Used to be hopes. But now it's all memories. Roche – I'm Totally Over You.'

Rochelle   I'm not listening to this.

Kitty   Roche. Stay.

Rochelle   No.

Kitty   But Roche –

Victor   And now Jay.

Rochelle   Why do we always listen to you, Kit? Why do we always do what you say?

Victor   What's your message to your ex, Jay?

Rochelle   We were happy. Me and H and Sin were happy with what you had.

Jake   I . . . Listen, I don't . . .

Kitty   No. But you wanted –

Rochelle   Don't tell me what I wanted. I wanted Dan. And I lost him and it's all your fault.

Victor   Come on, Jay. Don't be shy.

Exit **Rochelle**.

Victor   And what about you, Jay? What would you say?

Jake   I don't know. I . . .

Tyson   Jay . . . ?

Jake   If I was honest . . . I think I still miss her.

Kitty   Really?

Jake   So I suppose . . . no. I'm not over her.

Dan   Jay – that's not what we –

Kitty   So would you go out with her again if you had the chance?

Victor   All of the boys are single. Can we have another question?

Kitty   I wanna know. Would you like a second chance?

Jake   Maybe. I don't know.

Victor   Let's move on. Can we have another question?

Rubin   If you were a fruit, what kind of fruit would you be?

Kitty   I want an answer to my question.

Victor   What kind of fruit are you?

Framji   Guava.

Dan   Apricot.

Kitty   Jay. Jay. Answer my question.

Victor   I'm warning you. You'll be thrown out. Fruits. Tyson.

Tyson   Blueberry.

Kitty   Take her back, Jay.

Victor   If you were a fruit.

Jake   I. I . . . don't know.

Victor   What kind of fruit?

Kitty   Let him answer my question.

Victor   Okay. That's it. That's enough. Get her out.

Frenzy. Security guards descend on **Kitty**. *She struggles.*

Kitty   I just want to talk to Jay. Jay – please.

Victor   Get her out of here.

Kitty   Jay. Listen to me. This is Kitty. Will you take me back? I was wrong. How was I to know you were gonna be famous? Take me back, Jay, please.

Jake   Kitty. I can't –

Victor   Out. Out. Out. I want her out.

Finally, the security guards get the better of **Kitty** *and she is dragged out.*

As soon as **Kitty** *goes the mood of the room changes. Everyone stops playing their roles. (The press, security and stylists become* **Letitia**'s *drama class.)*

Tyson   What the freak you doing, Jay?

Jake   I don't know.

Framji   That's not the deal, Jay.

Jake   I know.

Tyson   Punish them. Hurt them. Teach them a lesson. That's what we said.

Jake   I know.

Tyson   So what the freak are you doing . . . ?

Jake   It just came out like that.

Framji   What is this? You want Kitty?

Jake   I think . . . Yes. I do.

Dan   But she doesn't want you, Jay.

Jake   She's chasing after me.

Dan   Because you're in Awesome.

Framji   She doesn't want the real you, Jake.

Jake   The real me?

Framji   You know. The one who goes to school and Burger King and listens to Korn.

Jake   Oh yeah, him.

Dan   The one who's not a celebrity.

Jake   But maybe if she thought I was a celebrity for a bit longer –

Tyson   No.

Jake   Oh come on. Just a bit more.

Framji   No way.

Jake   Maybe if she thinks I'm a celebrity and we get back together and then I tell her. Maybe then she'll see that –

Dan   Jay. We wanted to punish them. We've punished them. The story's over, okay?

Jake   Vic – please. Listen everybody. Just keep on pretending. Just keep on imagining, okay? It was great, wasn't it? Didn't you like it? Didn't you love it? Wasn't it better than school? Wasn't it better than drama class? You were all great. Freak me. You were fantastic. I totally believed you. Like you were the press and security guards. And the stylists – great. Brilliant. Yeah. Oh – and Victor. That manager. Do that manager again, Victor.

Victor   We're finished, Jay.

Jake   I want to see you do the manager again. And Letitia?

Letitia   Yeah?

Jake   Brilliant.

Letitia   Really?

Jake   I totally believed you. You want to be her some more?

Letitia   Well . . .

Jake   Go on. Everyone wants to do some more.

Victor   No. The play's over. The boys win and the lights go down. Thanks, everybody.

Jake   But what about me? I didn't win. I want Kitty. I want Kitty back.

Dan   Jay –

Jake   I love Kitty and I want her back.

Dan   Jay, you're embarrassing.

Jake   You've got to help me. All of you. You've all got to help me get Kitty.

Framji   She's not worth it, Jay.

Tyson   It's her put all these ideas in their heads in the first place.

Jake   I know.

Dan   It's her who told them all to chuck us.

Jake   I know.

Framji   It's her who only wants you cos she thinks you're in a boyband.

Jake   I know. But I still –

Dan   You tell her, Jay. You tell her what's really going on. And then you'll see what she's like.

Jake   Okay. Okay, I will

Framji   No boyband. No celebrity.

Jake   Okay. Okay.

Tyson   You'll tell her the truth?

Jake   I'll tell her the truth.

Tyson   Good luck.

Everyone exits apart from **Jake**, *who is left alone for a moment. Then* **Letitia** *re-enters.*

Letitia   I want to be my character again. Just a bit longer. It was so exciting. I mean, she's a boring person but still . . . I made up a whole biography and everything. Like I lost myself. I never had that happen before. I mean, I've been in plays and that. But I was always like, 'Look at me.' Or sometimes, 'I look terrible. Don't look at me.' And I'd always be looking over at my dad with the camcorder. But then, just now, I was gone. Like if I'd look in the mirror I wouldn't have recognised myself. Did you feel like that? When you were up there singing and you were pretending to be in that band? Wasn't pretending exciting?

Jake   Maybe. But – pretending. Isn't that lying?

Letitia   No. It's acting.

Jake   Which is lying.

Letitia   No. It's different.

Jake   How?

Letitia   I don't know. But it is.

Jake   I'm not gonna pretend or lie or act. I'm not gonna do any of that bullshit. I'm gonna tell her the truth.

Kitty *enters.*

Letitia   I better – I've got a lot to do. Check on the tour bus. They're very demanding. Videos, games, drinks. It all has to be right.

Jake   Stop it. Stop.

Letitia   We're doing a twenty-one-city tour. Europe. America's next month. But that's the music business. Ninety-nine per cent promotion. You can have the product –

Jake   Don't.

Letitia   But if you're not promoting you might as well not exist.

Jake   Shut up.

Letitia   I've got a lot of calls to make. Don't forget – *Smash Hits* at 3.30.

Jake   Please –

Exit **Letitia**.

Kitty   Do you have a stalker yet, Jay? Girl who doesn't sleep because she's thinking about you. Cries every time she sees your picture because she wants you so much. Some girls are like that.

Jake   So I hear. Kitty –

Kitty   Yeah. Some girls are really stupid.

Jake   Kitty –

Kitty   Did you mean that stuff?

Jake   What stuff?

Kitty   At the press conference. Jay. Will you go out with me?

Jake   I don't know.

Kitty   Let's be famous together, Jay. Let's wear the same clothes. Let's have matching tattoos. Let's be on the front pages together.

Jake   Kitty, listen, I don't wanna –

Kitty   Let's have an amazing wedding and cute kids and raise money for charity and –

Jake   Kit. There's something else I have to tell you.

Kitty   Yes?

Jake   I'm not . . . there's not . . . I sort of . . . I'm considering . . . I'm thinking about leaving the band.

Kitty   What?

Jake   I want to leave the band.

Kitty   Why?

Jake   Because we're not allowed girlfriends. So I have to make a choice. Drive around in the bus. Millions of girls screaming. See my face everywhere. Get very very rich. Be a celebrity all over the world. Or choose you. And then I saw you at the press conference and you were calling out to me – I've made a choice. Who wants freaking celebrity? I want Kitty.

Kitty   Is that true?

Jake   Yeah. That's totally true.

Kitty   But Jake. These people – parents, the kids at school, the teachers. They're all so boring. Do you want that?

Jake   S'pose not.

Kitty   When life could be exciting. I don't want to fit in, Jay. I want to stand out. Does that sound stupid to you?

Jake   No.

Kitty   And celebrities. They're not like us. Everything they do counts. When I read about that I'm so jealous. You can't just turn your back on celebrity.

Jake   But I've got all these feelings for you. And you've got all these feelings for me. That's more important. Will you go out with me, Kit?

Kitty   But I want to be famous. And I want you. I want both.

Jake   Choose, Kit. Decide.

Kitty   I can't choose.

Jake   You have to.

Kitty   But if I have to, I choose . . . celebrity.

Jake   Okay. Then – goodbye. I really – you know – really thought we were so like each other. But you're . . . we're so different, Kit. Goodbye.

Kitty   Did you really write that song?

Jake   Yeah, course.

Kitty   That song's gonna be huge. It's gonna be number one in markets all over the world.

Jake   You reckon?

Kitty   And Awesome are gonna fly everywhere, be everywhere, do everything, say everything. There's gonna be Pepsi, there's gonna be Cola, Macdonald's and then there's gonna be Awesome.

Jake   Yeah.

Kitty   You drive out into the bush or the jungle or the desert or something and show them pictures. What do they recognise? – Mickey Mouse, Madonna and Awesome. Jake – they're gonna be so famous it hurts. You've got to be part of that, Jake. You've got to sing the song.

Jake   But Kitty –

Kitty   Sing the song. Sing the song – and I'll love you.

Jake   Kitty –

Kitty   Yes?

Jake   I'm going back.

Kitty   You're – ?

Jake   I'm going back to the band. I'm going back to Awesome. I'm singing the song. I'm touring the world. I'm making the video. I'm going to be freaking famous.

Kitty   That's it, Jay. That's it. And me . . . ? Am I . . . ?

Jake   And you . . . and you're . . . and you're there with me, Kit. Every step of the way.

Kitty   Yes. Yes. Yes. Everywhere you go. Who's that girl? Who's that beautiful girl he's with? Of course we're going to have to handle it carefully. Your fans –

Jake   Want me single.

Kitty   But your management, your PR –

Jake   Will have to handle that.

Kitty   Because we love each other.

Jake   Yes. We love each other. And the fans will learn to accept –

Kitty   Will learn to love that.

Jake   Then we can be launched – rebranded – resold –

Kitty   A new start. Two dolls in the box. 'Kitty and Jake.'

Jake   Two faces on the covers. 'Kitty and Jake.'

Kitty   Two faces on the invites. 'Kitty and Jake.'

Jake   We're going to save the rainforests.

Kitty   We're going to save the planet.

Jake   We're going to shop for ever.

Kitty   We're going to love our fans.

Jake   But need our privacy.

Kitty   We'll sell shares in our future happiness.

Jake   We're going to promote, promote, promote.

Kitty   And spin and spin and spin.

Jake   Here and there and everywhere.

Kitty   And somewhere and nowhere. We're gods.

Jake   We're superstars.

Kitty   We're everything.

Enter **Rochelle** *and* **Dan**.

Rochelle   Has he told you yet, Kit? Has he told you the truth?

Kitty   What is this, Jake?

Jake Kitty. Maybe we should –

Rochelle It was all a trick, Kit. It was a game. To get us back.

Enter **Hannah** *and* **Tyson**.

Hannah Weren't they brilliant? They worked out the song and everything. Totally convincing.

Enter **Sinita** *and* **Framji**.

Sinita Excellent. So romantic.

Kitty Was this your idea?

Jake No. Victor's.

Enter **Victor** *and* **Letitia**.

Victor 'The future. The future, I see the future.'

Kitty Oh my God.

Letitia And I was playing the PA. That was me. Totally amazing. And this is the drama class.

The press, security and stylists all enter, wave and exit.

Letitia Fooled you. Isn't acting great?

Sinita Shall we all go to the movies? Who wants to see a film? Let's eat lots of popcorn and drink Coke.

Rochelle Diet Coke.

Sinita Diet Coke and watch a movie. Who's coming? Everybody? Come on.

Exit everyone apart from **Jake** *and* **Kitty**.

Kitty I always thought everyone else was thick. And I was clever. And I had to organise everyone. And if I didn't nothing would happen. But it was me. I'm the thick one.

Jake No.

Kitty   Yeah, stupid freaking stupid freaking idiot bitch to believe –

Jake   Kitty – don't –

Kitty   I just wanted to believe so much, so much – that stupid band, that song –

Jake   It's kind of funny. You could laugh.

Kitty   Yeah. I could laugh.

She cries. **Jake** *holds her.*

Kitty   You lied to me, Jake.

Jake   No. It was acting, pretending. Something.

Kitty   Why do boys never tell you what they feel? All the time I was going out I'd say, 'How you doing, Jay?' and you'd just be, 'Okay.' Tell me what you're feeling, Jay. Scared of a girl?

Jake   No.

Kitty   Then come on. Tell me the truth about how you feel.

Jake   The truth about how I feel. Okay. I feel everything for you, Kitty. I feel love. I feel kissing and cuddling and all that kind of love. But also like sex kind of love. Like I want to see you naked.

Kitty   Yeah?

Jake   And I feel hate. Like I want to scream and shout at you. Like I want to find all your weak points and really make you hurt.

Kitty   Really?

Jake   I feel like I want to spend the rest of my life with you. I feel like I never want to see you again. I feel like you're a supermodel. I feel like you're my sister. Or my mother. I feel like I want to tell everyone you're my girlfriend. I feel like I want to pretend I never knew you.

Kitty   God. Jacob.

Jake   What do you call it, Kit? When someone makes you have all these feelings? Is that love?

Kitty   I don't know.

Jake   Neither do I. What are you feeling now?

Kitty   I don't know.

Jake   Tell me. Scared of a boy? Tell me.

Kitty   I love you. I hate you. I want to kiss you. I want to scream at you. I want to stay with you. I want to run away from you. I – so much stuff.

Jake   It's bad, isn't it?

Kitty   It's terrible.

Enter **Victor**.

Victor   You coming to see the film?

Jake   I suppose. Kit. Do you wanna . . . ?

Kitty   I suppose.

Victor   Letitia asked me out.

Jake   That's nice.

Kitty   Great, Vic.

Victor   Aren't girls amazing?

Jake   Yeah. Amazing.

Kitty   What's the movie?

Victor   It's a comedy.

Jake/Kitty   Good.

End.

Methuen Drama Student Editions

Jean Anouilh *Antigone* • John Arden *Serjeant Musgrave's Dance*
Alan Ayckbourn *Confusions* • Aphra Behn *The Rover* • Edward Bond
Lear • *Saved* • Bertolt Brecht *The Caucasian Chalk Circle* • *Fear and
Misery in the Third Reich* • *The Good Person of Szechwan* • *Life of Galileo* •
Mother Courage and her Children • *The Resistible Rise of Arturo Ui* • *The
Threepenny Opera* • Anton Chekhov *The Cherry Orchard* • *The Seagull* •
Three Sisters • *Uncle Vanya* • Caryl Churchill *Serious Money* • *Top Girls*
• Shelagh Delaney *A Taste of Honey* • Euripides *Elektra* • *Medea* •
Dario Fo *Accidental Death of an Anarchist* • Michael Frayn *Copenhagen*
• John Galsworthy *Strife* • Nikolai Gogol *The Government Inspector* •
Robert Holman *Across Oka* • Henrik Ibsen *A Doll's House* • *Ghosts* •
Hedda Gabler • Charlotte Keatley *My Mother Said I Never Should* •
Bernard Kops *Dreams of Anne Frank* • Federico García Lorca *Blood
Wedding* • *Doña Rosita the Spinster* (bilingual edition) • *The House of
Bernarda Alba* • (bilingual edition) • *Yerma* (bilingual edition) • David
Mamet *Glengarry Glen Ross* • *Oleanna* • Patrick Marber *Closer* • John
Marston *Malcontent* • Martin McDonagh *The Lieutenant of Inishmore* •
Joe Orton *Loot* • Luigi Pirandello *Six Characters in Search of an Author*
• Mark Ravenhill *Shopping and F***ing* • Willy Russell *Blood Brothers*
• *Educating Rita* • Sophocles *Antigone* • *Oedipus the King* • Wole
Soyinka *Death and the King's Horseman* • Shelagh Stephenson *The
Memory of Water* • August Strindberg *Miss Julie* • J. M. Synge *The
Playboy of the Western World* • Theatre Workshop *Oh What a Lovely
War* Timberlake Wertenbaker *Our Country's Good* • Arnold Wesker
The Merchant • Oscar Wilde *The Importance of Being Earnest* •
Tennessee Williams *A Streetcar Named Desire* • *The Glass Menagerie*

Methuen Drama Modern Plays

include work by

Edward Albee
Jean Anouilh
John Arden
Margaretta D'Arcy
Peter Barnes
Sebastian Barry
Brendan Behan
Dermot Bolger
Edward Bond
Bertolt Brecht
Howard Brenton
Anthony Burgess
Simon Burke
Jim Cartwright
Caryl Churchill
Noël Coward
Lucinda Coxon
Sarah Daniels
Nick Darke
Nick Dear
Shelagh Delaney
David Edgar
David Eldridge
Dario Fo
Michael Frayn
John Godber
Paul Godfrey
David Greig
John Guare
Peter Handke
David Harrower
Jonathan Harvey
Iain Heggie
Declan Hughes
Terry Johnson
Sarah Kane
Charlotte Keatley
Barrie Keeffe
Howard Korder

Robert Lepage
Doug Lucie
Martin McDonagh
John McGrath
Terrence McNally
David Mamet
Patrick Marber
Arthur Miller
Mtwa, Ngema & Simon
Tom Murphy
Phyllis Nagy
Peter Nichols
Sean O'Brien
Joseph O'Connor
Joe Orton
Louise Page
Joe Penhall
Luigi Pirandello
Stephen Poliakoff
Franca Rame
Mark Ravenhill
Philip Ridley
Reginald Rose
Willy Russell
Jean-Paul Sartre
Sam Shepard
Wole Soyinka
Simon Stephens
Shelagh Stephenson
Peter Straughan
C. P. Taylor
Theatre de Complicite
Theatre Workshop
Sue Townsend
Judy Upton
Timberlake Wertenbaker
Roy Williams
Snoo Wilson
Victoria Wood

Methuen Drama Contemporary Dramatists
include

John Arden (two volumes)
Arden & D'Arcy
Peter Barnes (three volumes)
Sebastian Barry
Dermot Bolger
Edward Bond (eight volumes)
Howard Brenton
(two volumes)
Richard Cameron
Jim Cartwright
Caryl Churchill (two volumes)
Sarah Daniels (two volumes)
Nick Darke
David Edgar (three volumes)
David Eldridge
Ben Elton
Dario Fo (two volumes)
Michael Frayn (three volumes)
David Greig
John Godber (four volumes)
Paul Godfrey
John Guare
Lee Hall (two volumes)
Peter Handke
Jonathan Harvey
(two volumes)
Declan Hughes
Terry Johnson (three volumes)
Sarah Kane
Barrie Keeffe
Bernard-Marie Koltès
(two volumes)
Franz Xaver Kroetz
David Lan
Bryony Lavery
Deborah Levy
Doug Lucie

David Mamet (four volumes)
Martin McDonagh
Duncan McLean
Anthony Minghella
(two volumes)
Tom Murphy (six volumes)
Phyllis Nagy
Anthony Neilsen (two volumes)
Philip Osment
Gary Owen
Louise Page
Stewart Parker (two volumes)
Joe Penhall (two volumes)
Stephen Poliakoff
(three volumes)
David Rabe (two volumes)
Mark Ravenhill (two volumes)
Christina Reid
Philip Ridley
Willy Russell
Eric-Emmanuel Schmitt
Ntozake Shange
Sam Shepard (two volumes)
Wole Soyinka (two volumes)
Simon Stephens (two volumes)
Shelagh Stephenson
David Storey (three volumes)
Sue Townsend
Judy Upton
Michel Vinaver
(two volumes)
Arnold Wesker (two volumes)
Michael Wilcox
Roy Williams (three volumes)
Snoo Wilson (two volumes)
David Wood (two volumes)
Victoria Wood

Methuen Drama World Classics

include

Jean Anouilh (two volumes)
Brendan Behan
Aphra Behn
Bertolt Brecht (eight volumes)
Büchner
Bulgakov
Calderón
Čapek
Anton Chekhov
Noël Coward (eight volumes)
Feydeau
Eduardo De Filippo
Max Frisch
John Galsworthy
Gogol
Gorky (two volumes)
Harley Granville Barker
(two volumes)
Victor Hugo
Henrik Ibsen (six volumes)
Jarry

Lorca (three volumes)
Marivaux
Mustapha Matura
David Mercer (two volumes)
Arthur Miller (five volumes)
Molière
Musset
Peter Nichols (two volumes)
Joe Orton
A. W. Pinero
Luigi Pirandello
Terence Rattigan
(two volumes)
W. Somerset Maugham
(two volumes)
August Strindberg
(three volumes)
J. M. Synge
Ramón del Valle-Inclan
Frank Wedekind
Oscar Wilde

Methuen Drama Classical Greek Dramatists
include

Aeschylus Plays: One
(Persians, Seven Against Thebes, Suppliants,
Prometheus Bound)

Aeschylus Plays: Two
(Oresteia: Agamemnon, Libation-Bearers, Eumenides)

Aristophanes Plays: One
(Acharnians, Knights, Peace, Lysistrata)

Aristophanes Plays: Two
(Wasps, Clouds, Birds, Festival Time, Frogs)

Aristophanes & Menander: New Comedy
(Women in Power, Wealth, The Malcontent,
The Woman from Samos)

Euripides Plays: One
(Medea, The Phoenician Women, Bacchae)

Euripides Plays: Two
(Hecuba, The Women of Troy,
Iphigeneia at Aulis, Cyclops)

Euripides Plays: Three
(Alkestis, Helen, Ion)

Euripides Plays: Four
(Elektra, Orestes, Iphigeneia in Tauris)

Euripides Plays: Five
(Andromache, Herakles' Children, Herakles)

Euripides Plays: Six
(Hippolytos, Suppliants, Rhesos)

Sophocles Plays: One
(Oedipus the King, Oedipus at Colonus, Antigone)

Sophocles Plays: Two
(Ajax, Women of Trachis, Electra, Philoctetes)

For a complete catalogue
of Methuen Drama titles
write to:

Methuen Drama
36 Soho Square
London W1D 3QY

or you can visit our website at:

www.methuendrama.com